MICROWAVE
HINTS

D1608477

MICROWAVE
HINTS

Random Little Library
an imprint of
Random House Australia Pty Ltd
20 Alfred Street, Milsons Point NSW 2061

Sydney New York Toronto
London Auckland
and agencies throughout the world

Series Co-ordination: Gordon Cheers
Design: Liz Nicholson, Design Bite
Typeset by Axiom, 139 Charles Street, Abbotsford Vic 3067
Production by Vantage Graphics, Sydney
Printed by Australian Print Group, Maryborough

ISBN 0 09 182808 2

Information about recipe conversion is copyright © 1993
Sharp Corporation and is reproduced with permission.
Grateful thanks to Janelle Bloom of Sharp for her contribution.

Contents

THE MICROWAVE OVEN

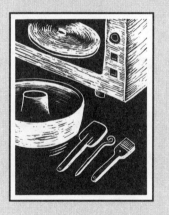

THE MICROWAVE OVEN

Microwave cooking saves time and energy and is also cleaner and healthier than conventional cooking. A microwave oven can be used as an accessory to back up your main stove or you could choose a combination oven, one that combines microwave cooking with conventional cooking.

This book is not intended to be a substitute for the manufacturer's instruction book that comes with your microwave oven. You must study that book in order to find out about how microwave ovens work, the differences between microwaves and conventional ovens and the basic techniques of microwave cookery.

The hints in this book are the result of experience and are intended to help you, once you have learned the basics, to make the most of this wonderful innovation the microwave oven.

Air circulation
Make sure that air can circulate around your microwave oven, and don't pile things on top of it.

Arcing
The use of too much foil, or metal touching foil, during microwave cooking will cause sparks inside the oven.

This is called arcing. If the amount of foil used is less than the amount of food and doesn't touch the walls or floor of the oven, arcing will not occur.

If arcing occurs, stop cooking and remove the foil. Arcing could damage the oven's magnetron if it occurs repeatedly.

Automatic programming
Automatic programming is a feature of some microwave ovens that allows more than one power setting to be programmed at once.

Alternatively you could program the oven to cook the food and have it ready when you come home, or defrost food and then cook it. However, this feature is no real advantage because microwave cooking is so fast and usually has to be watched anyway.

Browning dishes
Browning dishes are ideal for microwaving foods (such as bacon and eggs) that would normally be

fried. They are designed specifically for the microwave oven to sear and brown food in same way as conventional frying pans.

Browning dishes come in different shapes and sizes, and have a coated base that attracts microwave energy.

A browning dish must be preheated without food. Add food immediately the preheating is completed; do not allow the dish to cool. The food will absorb heat from the base and will brown.

To brown both sides it is necessary to turn the food on to the exposed area of the dish. For best results, press the food firmly on to the base for maximum contact with the heat of the dish.

HIGH (100%) is used for preheating the browning dish. Check the manufacturer's instructions for specific preheating times as the size of the dish will determine the length of preheating. Quantity and size of food will also affect preheating times.

If using oil or butter in the recipe, add them after preheating the browning dish, to prevent burning.

Don't use browning dishes in a conventional oven, on a hotplate or on a convection or combination cycle.

When cleaning a browning dish, do not use harsh abrasives or scourers because they will remove the metallic finish.

Burning
It is not possible to burn yourself on a microwave oven because the microwave energy switches off automatically when you open the door, and the oven itself does not get hot.

However, dishes do get hot because of the conduction of heat from the food being cooked in them, and browning dishes become very hot.

Buying a microwave oven
Buy a model larger than you think you will need. Once you find out how much you can do with a microwave oven, you will use it more than you thought you would at first.

Buy an established brand name.

A model with additional shelves may not be an advantage to you. Shelving increases the volume of food in the oven, but this then increases the cooking time and reduces the cooking speed.

A model with a browning element will be no

advantage to you if you already have a stove with a grill.

Choose a microwave oven with controls that you find easy to use and understand. They may be mechanical or digital touch controls.

China

China plates may be used for reheating food in a microwave oven. Avoid those with a metallic rim.

Cling film

Cling film is used to cover foods that could dry out, such as chicken or fish, and foods such as soups and stews that need to be simmered.

Make sure you use a brand that's marked 'microwave safe'.

Cling film also helps to keep vegetables moist without a lot of added fat or water. Corn on the cob, for example, will be moist and juicy when cling-wrapped individually and microwaved.

Cling film may be vented to prevent it splitting during cooking. Simply make a 2 cm slit in it with a sharp knife; this will help steam to escape.

When removing cling film be careful to lift it in such a way as to avoid steam burns.

Combination oven

A combination oven is one in which microwave and conventional energies are used simultaneously, or in sequence, in the same oven cavity.

An entire meal that looks as if it has been cooked traditionally can be produced very quickly.

Combination ovens are particularly good for roasting and baking, because the microwave energy provides speed combined with con-ventional browning.

Metal containers can be used in combination ovens, so that convenience foods can be defrosted and reheated in their foil containers, and normal cake tins and baking trays can be used.

Cookware shapes and sizes

Square and rectangular dishes tend to overcook in the corners so round containers are preferable for microwave cooking.

A square container could be used if you shield the corners with foil halfway through cooking.

Shallow dishes are more efficient than deeper ones, and straight-sided dishes are more efficient than angled ones.

Cookware types

Cookware that allows microwaves to be transmitted and is able to withstand the heat of the food is essential for microwave cooking.

To test the suitability of your existing cookware, place the utensil in the microwave oven beside a glass of water and microwave on HIGH for 1 minute. If the water is hot and the utensil is cold, the utensil is microwave-transparent and is suitable for microwave cooking.

If it is warm, it has absorbed microwave energy and is unsuitable for microwave cookery.

Use plastics marked 'microwave safe' and glassware marked 'oven-proof', 'heat resistant' or 'dishwasher safe'.

Cookware with moulded handles is best, because the glue of bonded or glued handles will disintegrate after prolonged use.

Metal dishes or china with a metal rim should not be used because metal causes arcing in the microwave oven.

Covers

A plate, lid, roasting bag or absorbent kitchen paper can all be used to cover food in the microwave oven.

Roasting bags should be pierced or slit to allow steam to escape and should be tied with non-metallic ties.

Cling film can be used if it is marked 'microwave safe', and foil should only be used for shielding.

Economy
Shorter cooking times and a lower electricity loading usually means that a microwave oven is cheaper to run than a conventional oven.

Foil
Because metal foil reflects microwave energy, it is generally not suitable for microwave cookery.

However, it can be used as a shielding agent.

Glass
Select only sturdy glass without a lead content for use in microwave ovens. Use for short cooking times and for reheating only.

Magnetron
This important component of the microwave oven converts the electric current into microwaves within the oven cavity.

Microwave oven
A microwave oven is an oven in which food is cooked by microwaves. Microwave ovens work more quickly than

conventional fuel ovens and use far less energy.

Microwave cooking takes roughly a quarter to a third of conventional cooking times, depending on the density of the food, its temperature at the start of cooking and the quantity of food being cooked.

Microwaves

Microwaves are high-frequency, short-wave, electromagnetic waves of energy. They penetrate about 5 cm into food where they are absorbed by water molecules. The molecules vibrate at great speed and the vibration generates heat by friction. Food further than 5 cm from the surface cooks by conduction of heat.

Movement

Don't move your microwave oven unnecessarily as movement could cause damage.

Paper towels

Paper towels are the best wrapping to use when you want crisp or dry results.

Grated coconut and breadcrumbs work well because the towel absorbs their moisture.

Fish should not be microwaved on paper towels because it can stick to them and be difficult to remove.

If you want a little more moisture but maximum air circulation, use a moist paper towel. Sandwiches and frozen muffins can be successfully warmed this way.

Use only white paper towels because coloured ones could bleed colour on to food.

Do not use recycled paper towels because recycled paper contains tiny traces of metal, which causes arcing in microwave ovens.

Plastic
Microwave-safe plastic cookware is suitable for most cooking methods in the microwave oven and

comes in a range of shapes and sizes.

Plate covers
Plate covers eliminate the need for cling film as a covering when reheating meals. They are dome-shaped and of microwave-safe plastic.

Pottery
Pottery is suitable for most cooking methods in the microwave oven provided it does not have a metallic glaze.

Power settings
See Variable power

Pyrex and pyro-ceramics
Both Pyrex and pyro-

ceramics are both micro-wave-transparent and heat-resistant, and can go from freezer to microwave oven to table.

Available in a variety of shapes and sizes, pyro-ceramics and Pyrex are suitable for all cooking methods.

Replacing the conventional oven

A microwave oven will not completely replace a conventional oven because microwaves have their limitations.

Some foods are better cooked in a conventional oven, and a microwave oven only holds a certain amount of food. But it is still an invaluable appliance, because it also cooks some food better than a conventional oven and has the great advantage of speed.

Roasting racks

A microwave roasting rack is useful for elevating meat and poultry above their own juices during cooking and thawing. It is also ideal for baking — a cake placed on a rack will cook better because the microwaves will circulate underneath the container.

A roasting rack should be made of pyro-ceramic or microwave-safe plastic.

The rack is placed in a microwave-safe roasting dish and the meat is laid on it.

Safety
There is no need to worry about the safety of microwave ovens. Microwaves are not produced unless the door is closed, and the doors are fitted with special locks, seals and safety cut-out switches which automatically switch the power off when the door is opened.

The ovens are also effectively sealed against the leakage of microwaves. Microwaves cannot escape in any way and they simply bounce around inside the oven.

Scales
Determining the weight of food is important when you are estimating cooking times, and it is necessary to have a pair of scales in your kitchen.

Shelves
If your microwave oven has a shelf that allows you to cook two things at once, remember that the top dish could shield the bottom one from cooking. So if you use both shelves, rotate the top and bottom dishes during cooking.

Standing time
Standing time is an

essential part of the microwave cooking and defrosting process in which the food is left to stand either inside or outside the oven.

Cooking or defrosting is completed during standing time by the conduction of the heat in the food to the centre.

Standing time will depend on the density and size of the food. For example, fish and vegetables require 2-3 minutes while roasts require 10-15 minutes.

Cover with a lid or foil to retain heat during standing.

Temperature probes

A temperature probe is a feature of some microwave ovens that enables you to judge cooking time by temperature.

The probe is inserted in the thickest part of the food and the other end is plugged into a special socket. When the desired temperature is reached, the oven turns itself off.

However, inserting a thermometer or other ways of checking whether food is cooked are generally more reliable.

Thermometers

The microwave ther-mometer replaces the

conventional meat ther-
mometer, which cannot be
used in microwave ovens
because of its mercury
content.

To make sure that bacteria
are destroyed, food should
be cooked or reheated to at
least 70°C throughout.

When checking the
temperature of food, allow
for standing time after
microwave cooking, which
helps the temperature to
even out, and measure the
temperature in several
positions. If the food isn't
hot enough, microwave the
food for another minute
before checking again.

To ensure that you get an
accurate reading with a

thermometer do not insert
it near any bone in a joint
of meat.

Turntable

A turntable in a microwave
oven turns the food
automatically during
cooking to ensure even
cooking. However, it is still
necessary to reposition
food manually.

Make sure that your
microwave cooking dishes
are not too big to prevent
the turntable from
working!

Variable power

Microwave cooking uses
time and variable power.
Variable power works
similarly to the temperature

settings on your conventional oven.

Of course, not all foods cook at the same temperature so different temperature settings are necessary. The same applies to the variable power on the microwave oven. Variable power control gives you a choice of different power levels, representing decreasing amounts of microwave energy.

Most microwave ovens feature five variable power levels:

HIGH (100%) is ideal for cooking vegetables, fruit, bacon and sauces, or reheating beverages.

MEDIUM HIGH (70%) is ideal for reheating leftovers and convenience foods or cooking casseroles and poultry.

MEDIUM (50%) is great for roasting meat and for cooking soups and stews, seafood and dairy products.

MEDIUM LOW (30%) is for defrosting and softening cream cheese, chocolate, butter, honey and ice-cream.

LOW (10%) is used to keep foods warm once they are cooked.

Waxed paper

Waxed paper should be used when you want to retain heat but let some moisture escape.

Some foods will be firmer when cooked if wrapped in waxed paper rather than cling film.

Waxed paper also prevents juicy foods, like tomato sauce, from splattering and for lining steamers so that tiny pieces of food don't fall through.

Another use for waxed paper is dry microwaving of foods that stick, such as fish fillets.

If your microwave oven has a fan the waxed paper might need to be tucked under a dish or heavy food so that it doesn't blow around.

Wood and cane
Some wooden items such as bamboo skewers or toothpicks can be used for kebabs or for securing rolled roasts.

TIPS AND TRICKS

Successful microwave cooking entails learning some new cooking techniques that characterise microwaving as well as adapting your existing techniques.

Because of the way microwaves work, such factors as the density, size or quantity of food cooked, the way food is arranged on a plate or dish and the temperature of food when cooking begins — among other things — affect the length of cooking time and the quality of your cooking.

It is also important to stir or turn food in order to even out cooking or increase exposure to microwaves. Other techniques, such as browning food on a special dish, elevating food on a rack and allowing food to stand for a few minutes after leaving the oven, must be added to your cooking procedures.

Other techniques common to conventional cooking, such as boiling or stir-frying, need to be adapted to microwave cooking in simple but important ways.

Arranging food

For best results, food to be microwaved should be arranged in a circle with the centre left empty, because this will allow the microwaves to penetrate the food from the centre as well as the outside, thus ensuring even cooking.

As microwaves are strongest from the outside edge, unevenly shaped foods such as chicken legs, broccoli and asparagus should be arranged with the inner parts or more delicate areas towards the centre.

Rearrange the food during cooking. For example, if cooking a dish of meat-balls, transfer the ones in the centre to the outside and vice versa.

Leave some space between pieces of food to allow microwave penetration from all sides.

Baby food

Baby food can be heated in a microwave as long as you take great care to ensure that the food does not become too hot for the baby.

Food can be heated on a low setting. Transfer the required amount from a jar to a small dish, stir it well and always check the temperature before serving.

Babies' milk should not be heated in a microwave once

it is in the feeding bottle, and microwaves are not suitable for sterilising feeding equipment, such as bottles and teats.

Baking

Cake and biscuit recipes need to be adapted for successful cooking in a microwave oven.

A plastic cake container will not need greasing unless the mixture contains very little fat.

However, the base of large containers should be lined with greaseproof paper.

Since cakes sometimes do not cook properly in the middle, a ring mould is the best type of container to use for microwave cooking.

Cake mixtures must be no more than half full before cooking.

Cakes should be elevated on a microwave roasting rack to enable microwaves to penetrate evenly.

Cakes cooked in a microwave oven will not brown as they do when cooked conventionally. However, there are ways of adding colour to them, such as using brown sugar and wholemeal flour.

Most biscuits cannot be cooked in a microwave oven because they can only be cooked in small batches and because they need to be turned often.

However, biscuit slices – cooked in one slab in a slice tin and cut into pieces after cooking – are ideal for microwave cooking.

For further, more specific hints, see the chapter on cakes and desserts later in this book.

Boiling
A microwave oven can be used to boil vegetables, pasta and rice, and less water is needed than in conventional cooking.

Always use a large container, and never fill any bowl more than two-thirds full, so that liquids can boil without spilling over the top.

Space is also required for stirring.

Cover the container with a large plate or lid. Do not use cling film unless it is marked 'microwave safe'.

Boiling water
To boil water in a micro-wave oven, put the water in a bowl or jug in the oven and set the oven on HIGH.

If you need more than 300 ml of water, however, it will be quicker and more economical to boil the water in an electric kettle.

Bone

Bone is an excellent conductor of heat, so much so that it will cause the surrounding meat to overcook.

Boneless cuts of meat will cook more evenly than cuts with the bone in.

Browning

Heat the empty browning dish on HIGH for 5-8 minutes or according to the manufacturer's instructions.

For a crisp brown surface, brush the dish with oil after preheating — but no more than 2 tablespoons.

Do not remove the browning dish from the oven as it will cool quickly. Add the oil and food to the dish as it sits in the oven.

The browning dish becomes very hot, so always handle it with oven gloves.

Use tongs when positioning the food on the browning dish so that the oil will be less likely to splatter.

Butter

Butter taken straight from the refrigerator can be softened in a microwave oven by cooking it on LOW for 30-60 seconds.

To melt butter, cut it into small cubes, place it in a small bowl and cook on HIGH until melted

(30 seconds to 2 minutes, depending on quantity).

To clarify butter, cook 150 g butter in a microwave-safe jug on MEDIUM LOW for 6 minutes or until the butter begins to foam. Remove the foam and leave the remaining butter to stand for 5 minutes.

Use in recipes requiring clarified butter or ghee.

Children

The microwave oven is safe for children to use because of the absence of direct heat or gas burners and the automatic switching off when the door is opened.

However, because the dishes can get hot, children should be taught to use oven gloves.

Cleaning

The inside of a microwave oven must be cleaned after every use as any spilled food will absorb microwave energy and slow down cooking time. Simply wipe the inside with a damp cloth.

If the walls become heavily soiled, place a bowl of water in the oven and heat on HIGH to boiling point. The steam thus produced will soften stubborn dirt.

Do not use abrasive cleaners as they will damage the oven's surfaces.

See also Smells

Coffee beans

Stale coffee beans can be revived by placing them on a paper towel and micro-waving for 30 seconds on HIGH. Rearrange the beans after 15 seconds.

Cooking problems

If food cools quickly, it might not be cooked through or it might be cooked unevenly. Try covering the food during standing time, then cooking for another 2-3 minutes.

If food boils over, either the container is too small or the food cooked too fast. Try using a different type of container or a container twice the volume of the food, and try buttering or oiling the upper rim of the container.

If food looks different from when you cook it conventionally, it is because it cooks too quickly in the microwave oven to brown and because there is no external heat to brown it.

Try using browning agents or toppings for meat (see the meat and poultry chapters for hints).

For cakes and biscuits, add dark-coloured spices to the mixture, and use whole-meal flour and brown sugar.

If food cooks to slowly, it could be that your electrical circuit is overloaded.

If meat is tough, either the power setting is too high or the meat was salted before cooking. Try reducing the power level in future; don't salt meat before cooking but only when ready to serve; and marinate less tender cuts of meat before cooking.

If a cake remains uncooked in the centre, perhaps the cooking and/or standing times were too short, or the dish was too large.

In future, allow a cake to cool, loosely covered, for 10-15 minutes on a flat surface, and cook cakes in a round dish or ring mould, elevated on a microwave roasting rack.

If eggs are tough and rubbery, the power setting was probably too high.

Use a lower setting for delicate foods like eggs.

If cheese is tough and springy, the power setting was too high and a lower setting should have been used. It is also a good idea to add cheese later in the cooking time.

Cooking time

Microwave ovens vary considerably in their power output (from 650 watts to 800-900 watts) and therefore cooking times also vary.

The times suggested in this book must be regarded as

indications only, and you are advised to study the instruction book for your model.

Always check food at the minimum suggested cooking time and return to the oven for more cooking if necessary.

Some foods cook more quickly than others in the microwave oven. For example, foods with high fat or sugar content will cook and reheat more quickly than those which are low in these ingredients.

Also, food with a high moisture content will take longer to cook or reheat than drier foods.

Other factors will also vary the required cooking time, including the quantity of food, whether the ingredients are warm or cold, whether the oven was cold or warm when you started cooking, and the type of cookware used.

Covering food

In order to prevent drying out, foods such as soups, fish, vegetables and fruit should be covered to retain their moisture. Foods that require constant attention, such as sauces and scrambled eggs, and dry foods, such as pastries, should not be covered.

If a 'dry' result is required (e.g. roasting or cooking

small cuts of meat in a browning dish), covering is unnecessary. Prevent splatter by covering the dish with absorbent paper towelling, which will allow steam to escape.

Even when food is covered to retain its moisture, some steam should escape. This will prevent pressure build-up. Lids should be well fitting but not tight. Use a plate or pierced cling film as a cover.

Cream cheese

Cream cheese can be softened by placing it in a microwave oven on the DEFROST setting until soft enough for spreading.

Density

Food of the same size but different densities will cook at different rates; for example, if a roast and a meatloaf are the same size, the meatloaf will cook faster. The rate of conduction of heat to the centre of the meatloaf is faster than that to the roast because the meatloaf is the less dense of the two.

Defrosting

One of the best things about microwave ovens is the speed and ease with which they defrost frozen food. See the chapter on defrosting.

Elevating

Elevating large items of

food such as roasts and cakes allows better microwave penetration to occur from underneath the food, promoting even and faster cooking. To elevate food, use a specially designed rack or an upturned saucer.

Fat content

Fat attracts more microwaves than meat. This means that meat with fat on will cook more slowly than meat without, because the microwaves will be attracted from the meat to the fat. In addition, the meat directly in contact with the fat will overcook.

It is important, therefore, to trim as much fat as possible from meat intended for microwave cooking.

Food temperature

Food taken straight out of the refrigerator will take longer to cook in a microwave oven than food at room temperature.

Health

Cooking in the microwave oven minimises vitamin and mineral losses, because the foods are cooked quickly in small amounts of water or their own juices, which means that there is less likelihood that vitamins and minerals will leach out and be lost in the cooking water.

Microwave cooking is less fatty, because deep-frying is not possible and fat must be trimmed off meat to ensure even cooking.

Microwaving makes it much easier to prepare high-fibre foods such as beans, cracked wheat, hot cereals and vegetables.

Foods that help to defend the body against cancer, such as cabbage, broccoli, brussels sprouts, dark leafy greens and spinach, all cook well in the microwave oven, which retains their colour, flavour and nutrients.

Hot and cold spots

Some microwave ovens have hot or cold spots, areas where food will cook faster or slower than elsewhere. To overcome these spots, reposition food during cooking.

Limitations

There is very little indeed that cannot be cooked in a microwave oven or for which a microwave oven is not very suitable. However, there are some definite don'ts.

Boiled eggs will explode if cooked in a microwave unless wrapped in aluminium foil.

Deep-frying should not be attempted as it is not possible to control the temperature of the oil.

Yorkshire pudding, choux pastry, soufflés and conventional meringue mixture will not rise, and roast potatoes and parsnips will not brown in a microwave.

Large rich fruit cakes need long slow cooking and are not suitable for microwave ovens.

Batter will not become crisp in a microwave, and large turkeys will not fit.

Oven bags
Use oven bags for roasting and pot roasting meat.

Do not use metal twist ties; secure the oven bag with a rubber band or string. (Some brands of oven bag now come with plastic ties for microwave use.) Pierce the bag to prevent bursting.

Pierce
Because food cooks quickly in the microwave oven, the build-up of steam or pressure can be great.

It is important, therefore, to pierce the skins of foods such as jacket potatoes, tomatoes and sausages to prevent them bursting.

Poaching and steaming
To poach or steam food in a microwave oven, chop the food into evenly sized

pieces and place them in a large, shallow dish.

Add the amount of liquid stated in the recipe, and cover with a tightly fitting lid or a heavy plate.

Because food cooks in its own moisture, less liquid is needed than when poaching or steaming conventionally.

Stir or reposition the food during cooking.

Porridge
Put about 50 g porridge oats (for two people) and 300 ml of milk in a deep bowl.

Cook on high for 4-5 minutes until boiling and thickened, stirring every minute.

Position
Because the pattern of microwave energy is more concentrated around the outside rather than the centre of the microwave oven, food must be positioned towards the outside to maximise microwave absorption.

If cooking a large, unevenly shaped cut of meat such as a leg of lamb, position the largest portion towards the outside.
See also Arranging food

Power levels and uses
HIGH (100% of power output) is used for boiling

water, cooking fresh fruit and vegetables, heating non-milk drinks, cooking confectionery and pre-heating a browning dish.

MEDIUM (70%) is used for cooking fish and shellfish, cakes, meats, poultry, eggs and cheeses.

MEDIUM-LOW (55%) is used for cooking custards, melting butter and chocolate, and cooking casseroles.

LOW (30%) is used for cooking less tender cuts of meat, simmering soups and stews, and softening butter and cream cheese.

WARM (10%) is used for keeping foods warm,

proofing yeast, softening ice cream and making yoghurt.

DEFROST (35%) is used for thawing frozen foods.

STAND/TIMER (on some models) (0%) is used to start cooking at a later time, to program standing time after cooking and as a reminder timer.

Problems with the microwave oven

No power: Is your oven plugged in?

Check your fuse or circuit breaker.

Oven not operating: Is the oven door closed? Are the controls set properly?

Cooking takes longer than time in the cookbook: Have you selected the correct power? Is there low voltage at the power outlet?

The starting temperature and shape of foods vary, so cook a little longer.

Uneven cooking, or under- or overcooking: Is the food incorrectly wrapped, or have you used an incorrect container? are the controls set properly? For large pieces of meat, utilise standing time at room temperature after cooking.

Oven light flickers: This is normal.

Water condensation around the oven door: This is normal – wipe dry.

Sparks occur: There must be a metallic wrap or container touching the oven wall. The dish or glassware might be trimmed with metal or the container has metal parts or rim.

Recipe conversion

Many conventional recipes can be adapted to microwave cooking with few changes other than a shortened cooking time. Your best guide is a microwave recipe for a similar type of food.

Compare the amount and type of main bulky ingredients and liquid.

If they are similar, use the container, cooking

techniques, power level and time recommended in the microwave recipe to convert your conventional recipe.

Watch the food carefully, and check for doneness after the minimum time.

If longer cooking is needed, add more time in small amounts. Be sure to allow standing time for foods which require it.

Moist foods, like chicken, seafood, minced beef, vegetables, fruits and saucy main dishes or casseroles, convert well. Dry or crusty foods may have a moist surface when microwaved.

Techniques like covering, steaming and stirring are common to both conventional and microwave cooking.

A recipe that calls for these techniques should convert easily and give excellent results when microwaved.

No change in ingredients should be needed for foods which are heated rather than cooked, such as dips, spreads and some casseroles, or foods which are brought to a boil but not simmered, like white sauce or pudding.

Reduce liquid in recipes that call for raw ingredients, simmering or baking longer than is needed to heat food through.

Little evaporation occurs during microwaving. Use two-thirds the liquid and add more, if needed, as you cook.

Omit fat needed to brown foods and prevent sticking in conventional cooking. A small amount of butter or olive oil may be used for flavour.

Use less salt or highly flavoured seasonings, like garlic, chilli, curry powder or sage. After microwaving, correct seasoning to taste. Small amounts of mild herbs and spices need not be changed.

Power level depends on the type of food to be microwaved. See your oven's instruction book. Add delicate or quick-cooking ingredients, like seafood and cheese, towards the end of microwaving to avoid toughening them.

Cooking time depends on the quantity and type of foods, so a comparable microwave recipe is your most accurate guide.

Microwaving time may be a quarter to a third of conventional time.

Check for doneness frequently and add more time in small amounts.

Change dish size and cooking time when you change the yield of a microwave recipe. Whether you double a recipe or cook half of it, the level of food should be the same depth as the original microwave recipe.

If food is spread too thinly, it will overcook or dry out. It will boil over if the dish is too full.

To double a recipe, double the ingredients, then decrease liquid by a quarter to a third; increase time by half to two-thirds.

For half a recipe, use half the ingredients and cut time by a third.

Reheating

Microwave ovens can reheat food wonderfully fast. See the chapter on reheating.

Roasting

Large joints of meat cannot be cooked in a microwave oven because the microwaves cannot reach the centre of the joint without the outside becoming overcooked.

Smaller joints, however, can be roasted successfully.

Boned and rolled meats cook more evenly when roasted in the microwave because the shape and thickness are uniform.

A microwave roasting rack must be used so that juices will drain away and microwaves will be able to penetrate more evenly.

Using an oven bag is a good idea because it

prevents splattering. However, it must be pierced so that steam can escape.

A joint should be turned at least once during roasting to ensure even cooking.

Standing time after cooking must be allowed. The joint should be covered or wrapped in foil during standing time to prevent loss of heat.

Roasts cooked in a microwave do not colour as in conventional cooking, so you have to check the colour of the meat juices when testing for doneness.

Rotating

Although modern microwave ovens are equipped with either a turntable or stirrer fan, it is still necessary to rotate large dishes halfway through cooking.

The easiest way to do this is to move the dish to the opposite side of the oven.

Service

If you use your microwave oven correctly and do not move it about frequently or drop it, there is no need for it to be checked, and it will give you years of service.

However, if a service is required, it should only be carried out by a qualified technician from the manufacturing company.

Shape

Irregularly shaped food will cook unevenly, whatever the cooking method. The shank end of a leg of lamb, for example, will cook faster than the rest of the leg, because it is thinner.

To overcome this, asked the butcher to bone-out the leg and roll it into a uniform shape.

Alternatively, shield the shank end from microwave energy by covering it with a piece of foil. As metal reflects microwaves, this will slow down the cooking of the shielded part.

Shielding

Shielding is the process of protecting vulnerable parts of food in order to prevent overcooking.

The thin ends of meat, poultry and fish should be shielded with smooth strips of aluminium foil.

Shielding can also be useful when using a square or rectangular container to prevent the corners from overcooking, such as when cooking loaf cakes.

It's a good idea then to cover the dish with grease-proof paper or cling film to prevent arcing.

Size

Large pieces of food take longer to cook than smaller pieces of food.

This is because smaller pieces receive almost total microwave penetration, whereas larger items rely on the conduction of heat from the outer to the inner area.

Smells

To remove unwanted smells from your microwave oven, place the juice and peel of a lemon in a bowl with 2-3 cups water.

Microwave on HIGH for 5 minutes, then wipe the inside of the oven with a damp cloth.

Browning dishes can retain smells from previous cooking. Make a paste of baking soda and lemon juice and rub it over the surface. Cover with a wet paper towel and let it soak for about an hour, then wash.

Stains

Some plastic-type microwave cookware stains easily from the foods cooked in it.

To remove these stains, mix baking soda and lemon juice into a paste and rub it into the surface.

Cover with a damp paper towel and allow to sit before washing.

Standing

Standing is a technique used to complete cooking out of the microwave oven.

Although microwave absorption ceases at the end of cooking, vibration continues, reducing gradually.

While this vibration continues, so does heat conduction, providing food is kept covered.

Sterilising jam jars

A microwave oven can be used to sterilise jam jars. Quarter-fill up to four jars with water. Arrange them in a circle in the oven, then bring to the boil on HIGH.

Using oven gloves, remove each jar as it is ready and pour out the water. Invert the jar on a clean tea towel or kitchen paper and use as required.

Stir-frying

Stir-frying can be done successfully in a microwave oven because only a small quantity of fat is used.

Choose foods that cook quickly, such as tender cuts of meat, chicken and vegetables. See also the chapter on meat.

Stirring

Stirring rearranges food to take advantage of microwave concentration.

This helps conduct the microwaves quickly and evenly to the food and is useful for casseroles and meat sauces.

Since the outer edges of food normally cook first in

a microwave oven, stir from the outside of the dish towards the centre. Foods that cannot be stirred (such as chicken pieces) should be turned over at least once during cooking.

Temperature

The colder the food at the start of cooking, the slower the conduction of heat to the centre. A dinner plate from the fridge will take longer to reheat than one at room temperature.

Timing

Using a microwave oven for cooking saves you a lot of time, but you will have to rearrange the order in which you cook various dishes.

You should also set the table and prepare the salad (if applicable) before putting food in the microwave oven.

See also Cooking time *(above)*

Turning

When practical, large items of food should be turned over at least once during cooking. This technique is generally only used for roasting or when browning both sides of small cuts of meat in the browning dish.

Warm plates

To warm plates, place a wet piece of kitchen towel between each plate and microwave them for 2 minutes on HIGH.

MEAT

Meat, offal and game can be cooked successfully in a microwave oven with great savings in time and energy.

There are certain basic principles to be observed. For example, do not add salt before cooking because it draws out the juices and makes the meat tough. Always elevate joints on a roasting rack so that the juices drain away, rather than accumulating and slowing down cooking. For best results always bring meat to room temperature before cooking. Standing time of 10-15 minutes should be allowed after cooking. Meat cut into small pieces or thin strips will cook more quickly than larger pieces.

There are also certain limitations to microwave meat cookery, but this chapter tells you how they can be overcome. Meat does not brown, so if colour is desired, a baste will have to be used.

Bacon

Remove the rind from bacon rashers and snip the fat with scissors to prevent it curling up during cooking.

Lay the bacon in a single layer on a roasting rack or a large flat plate. Cover with absorbent kitchen paper to absorb the fat and prevent splattering. Microwave on HIGH until cooked.

(Two rashers will take 2-2$\frac{1}{2}$ minutes, four rashers 4-4$\frac{1}{2}$ minutes, six rashers 5-6 minutes.)

Remove the paper quickly to prevent it sticking to the bacon.

Browning meat

When browning meat on a microwave browning dish don't cover it or it will steam instead of browning.

Before cooking a roast or casserole, seal and brown the meat first, either in a frying pan or on the hot-plate in a casserole dish.

There are many ways in which meat can be browned when cooked in a microwave oven.

A simple aid to browning is to dry meat with paper towels before cooking.

Commercial browning agents are available for specific microwave use.

Ham can be brushed with jellies, preserves, glazes or marmalades halfway through cooking time.

Brown meats for roasting with orange juice, red-currant jelly and dried mint.

Small quantities of dried herbs or spices mixed with melted unsalted butter or oil give additional colour.

Using oven bags when roasting improves the colour of the meat. (Remember to pierce the bag.)

Cook sausages, chops and steak in a browning dish.

Worcestershire, soy, teriyaki, barbecue, tomato, satay, tandoori or steak sauces brushed over meat will add colour as well as flavour.

Gravy or dry soup mixes will brown and flavour meat when rubbed over the surface.

Spices such as paprika will provide colour and flavour.

Parisienne or coffee essence will give colour. So will coffee powder mixed with lemon juice or water.

Casseroling
The microwave is the ideal way to cook up creative casseroles. They are ready in a fraction of the time of a conventional oven and retain both the flavour and

the texture of traditional recipes.

Trim off any fat and cut the meat into small cubes or strips. The bone-in cuts should be left whole. Preheat a casserole browning dish on HIGH for 8 minutes. Then quickly add 2 teaspoons oil, the meat and 500 g cubed vegetables; stir to ensure even browning.

Alternatively, brown the meat and vegetables in a microwave-safe, ovenproof casserole dish on a hotplate. Add ½ cup liquid (stock or wine), cover and cook.

After cooking, thicken the juices with a little blended cornflour. Cook meat for a further 3-5 minutes on the designated power setting.

Casserole cooking and standing times

Beef stew (using 500 g meat) should cook on HIGH for 5 minutes then on MEDIUM for 45 minutes. Allow to stand for 10 minutes.

Lamb casserole (using 500 g tender meat, e.g. lamb fillets) should cook on HIGH for 5 minutes then on MEDIUM for 20 minutes. Allow to stand for 10 minutes.

Lamb stew (using 500 g less tender meat, e.g.

mutton) should be cooked for 5 minutes on HIGH then for 50-60 minutes on LOW.

Pork casserole (using 500 g meat) should be cooked for 6-8 minutes on HIGH, then for 7-9 minutes on MEDIUM. Allow to stand for 20 minutes.

Veal stew (using 500 g meat) should be cooked for 10 minutes on HIGH, then on MEDIUM for 35 minutes. Allow to stand for 5 minutes.

Casserole liquids
The quantity of liquid required in a microwave-cooked casserole is generally a third less than

a conventionally cooked casserole.

Start with hot liquid if possible in order to reduce cooking time.

Casseroling vegetables
Always pre-cook hard vegetables (such as carrots, onions or potatoes) before adding the meat. Cook the vegetables in a covered casserole dish without water until they are just becoming tender. This procedure will avoid having undercooked vegetables in the finished casserole.

Chicken liver
Trim, halve and wash the livers and pat dry with

kitchen towels. Then prick them with a toothpick to prevent bursting during cooking.

Place 25 g butter in a dish and melt by heating on HIGH for 45 seconds. Add 250 g chicken livers, cover and cook on HIGH for 2-3 minutes, stirring once. Leave to stand for 2 minutes.

Defrosting

Always ensure that frozen joints of meat are completely defrosted before cooking.

Frying

A microwave oven can be used for frying and stir-frying, but **deep-frying**

must not be attempted because the temperatures are not constant and cannot be controlled.

A browning dish is essential for frying.

Trim steaks or chops of any fat. Preheat the browning dish. Quickly smear a little oil over half the dish, then firmly press the meat on to the oiled half of the base. Cook on MEDIUM HIGH until the meat is cooked (about 2-3 minutes per steak or chop). When meat is almost cooked, smear the other half of the browning dish with a little oil. Turn meat over to seal and brown on the other side.

Kebabs

It is important to use wooden skewers for kebabs rather than metal ones to prevent arcing.

Trim excess fat from lamb and cut into cubes. Thread on to skewers and brown before cooking.

Cook lamb kebabs on MEDIUM HIGH for 6-8 minutes, turning halfway through cooking time.

Kidney

To stop kidneys from popping and splattering during cooking, prick each kidney twice with a fork. Alternatively, chop them finely. Covering them during cooking is also a good idea.

Melt 25 g butter in a microwave-safe dish and then add the kidneys. Cover and cook on HIGH for 3-4 minutes for 250 g and 6-8 minutes for 500 g, stirring halfway through the cooking time. Stand for 3 minutes. When cooked kidneys should be slightly tinged with pink in the centre.

Lamb chops

Marinate lamb chops in equal quantities of soy sauce and honey before cooking.

Elevate the chops in the oven and cook uncovered. Allow about 2 minutes per chop on MEDIUM power.

Liver

Timing is critical when cooking liver because it becomes hard and grainy if overdone.

To cook liver, remove skin and any tough membranes. Cook in a browning dish which has been preheated for 5 minutes and add a little oil, pressing the liver down into it. Cook 250 g liver on high for 3-4 minutes and 500 g for 6-7 minutes, turning halfway through cooking time. Cover and allow to stand for 3 minutes.

Pig and ox liver may also be cooked slowly in a sauce for a further 25-30 minutes on MEDIUM until tender. *See also* Chicken liver

Marinating

When marinating meat for extra flavour, drain thoroughly and pat dry with paper towels to prevent splattering when placing on a preheated browning dish.

Meatballs

Arrange meatballs in a circle in a dish to ensure even cooking, and try to leave a space in the middle so that microwaves can penetrate from the inner as well as the outer edges.

Meatloaf

Always elevate the dish to ensure that the meatloaf cooks underneath.

Meatloaf is cooked when it shrinks slightly from the

sides of the dish and the centre is slightly under-cooked (standing time allows the centre to complete cooking).

Mince
Finely ground lean mince produces best results in a microwave oven. If using coarsely ground mince, however, reduce the power setting and increase the cooking time to ensure a tender result.

To fry mince, preheat a browning casserole dish on HIGH for 8 minutes. Add mince and stir. Cook mince on HIGH for 2-3 minutes, stirring occasionally. Drain excess fat and liquid from cooked mince.

When cooking savoury mince, use less liquid than you normally would. The amount of liquid you begin with is the amount you will end up with.

When cooking mince, drain off juices as they accumulate.

Chopped onion and garlic need not be fried when using a microwave oven. They can be mixed with the mince before cooking to add flavour.

Offal *See* Chicken liver, Kidney, Liver, Oxtail

Oven bags
When using an oven bag for roasting, add vegetables

and herbs such as onions, carrots, celery and parsley to the bag to enhance the flavour of the meat.

Utilise any juices that accumulate for gravy.

Cooking meat in an oven bag improves browning.

Oxtail

Oxtail needs very long, slow cooking in liquid to tenderise it and is best cooked the day before serving. Refrigerate the dish so that the fat sets on the surface and can then be removed.

Cook 1 kg oxtail in a browning dish (which has been preheated for 5 minutes), press the tail

down and cook on HIGH for 6-8 minutes. Transfer to a dish and add onions, carrots, celery and stock. Cover and cook on MEDIUM for about 1 hour or until tender, stirring during cooking. Stand for 10 minutes.

Pheasant

Choose a young bird for roasting because older ones are likely to be tough. Cover with rashers of bacon before cooking.

Place a knob of butter in the body cavity of a 900 g pheasant. Place the bird breast side down in a roasting dish and cover with a split roasting bag. Cook on MEDIUM for 7-8 minutes per 500 g and turn over halfway through cooking. Shield any parts that may overcook with foil. Cover and allow to stand after cooking for 5 minutes.

Pork

If pork is dry and tough after microwave cooking, it is overcooked.

Make use of standing time to achieve evenly cooked, tender and moist results.

The finished temperature of microwaved pork should always be checked with a thermometer. It should read 77°C.

Position

Position cuts of meat so that the thickest parts are pointing towards the edge of the dish.

Pot roasting

Marinate meat overnight in red wine, if desired, before pot-roasting.

Drain well before browning.

To pot roast in a micro-wave oven, trim the meat of any fat. Preheat a large, deep browning dish on HIGH (100%) for about 10 minutes.

Add the meat, turning to brown on all sides.

Alternatively, brown the meat on a hotplate in a microwave-safe, ovenproof casserole dish.

Add 1 cup stock, $^1/_3$ cup red wine, bay leaves, 1 quartered onion and peppercorns. Insert a microwave-safe meat thermometer into the thickest portion.

Cover and cook on MEDIUM LOW, allowing 15 minutes per 500 g for medium (internal temperature 55°C), 18 minutes per 500 g meat for well done (internal temperature 65°C).

To ensure even cooking, elevate the casserole dish and turn meat halfway through cooking.

Stand, covered, until internal temperature reaches 60-65°C for medium or 70-75°C for well done. Thicken the juices with blended corn-flour to make gravy.

Pot roasts cook perfectly in oven bags.

Quail

Each quail weighs about 150 g so allow 1-2 birds per person. To prevent the flesh from drying out, wrap the bird in bacon. Secure the legs to the body with wooden toothpicks.

Place 4 quail in a pierced roasting bag, then place them in a dish and cook on HIGH for 6-8 minutes. Turn once during cooking. Allow to stand for 2 minutes. To enhance their colour, place them under a grill during the standing time.

Rabbit
To microwave a 1 kg rabbit, arrange the pieces around the rim of a large glass pie dish.

The meaty parts of the legs should point outwards and the bony parts should point towards the middle.

Tuck the thin sides of the saddle under the thicker part so that they don't overcook.

Cover with cling film, pierce it and microwave on MEDIUM until cooked through — about 20-25 minutes.

Rotate the dish and turn the pieces about halfway through.

Allow the dish to stand for about 5 minutes before serving.

Recipe conversion
Cuts that you normally braise or stew should be microwaved with liquid in a covered container. Some conventional pot roasts call for enough liquid to cover the meat; use only the amount needed for the gravy.

To convert main dishes and casseroles, choose recipes for moist or saucy foods that call for covering, stirring or steaming.

Cooking time depends on quantity, size of pieces and type of ingredients.

Casseroles made with precooked ingredients may take as little as a quarter of the conventional time.

Your best guide is a microwave recipe for a similar amount and type of food.

Roasting basics

Large joints of meat cannot be cooked in a microwave oven because the micro-waves cannot reach the centre of the joint without the outside being over-cooked.

However, small joints can be roasted successfully.

Boned and rolled meats cook more evenly when roasted in the microwave because the shape and thickness are uniform.

When roasting meat, use a roasting rack to keep the juices from the underside of the meat and to elevate the meat so that microwaves will be able to penetrate all over.

For even cooking, joints of meat should be uncovered and turned at least once during cooking.

A piece of paper towel or a split oven bag could be used as a cover to reduce splattering.

Roast meat is cooked when the juices run clear. Always

cook for the minimum time suggested, allow to stand, test with a skewer and return to the oven for further cooking if necessary.

Season meat at the end of cooking, never beforehand, because salt drains the moisture from the meat and makes it dry. The only exception is when cooking pork crackling.

Standing time must be allowed. Remove the roast from the oven, cover or wrap it in foil to keep it warm while you prepare the rest of the meal, and allow the roast to stand for the time specified in the recipe.

See also Roasting procedure, Roasting times

Roasting procedure

Trim meat of any fat, and weigh it to calculate the cooking time. Tie the joint with string to make it as even as possible.

Elevate the meat and, if using a microwave-safe thermometer, insert it in the thickest portion away from the bone. If desired, brush meat with a browning agent.

Shield those areas of meat that will start to cook too quickly.

Remove the juices as they accumulate.

Turn the roast at least once during cooking.

When the calculated cooking time has elapsed, check the meat thermometer. If the correct internal cooking temperature has been reached, remove roast from the oven and stand, covered, until the correct internal standing temperature has been reached.

If you are using a conventional thermometer, insert it in the roast after the estimated cooking time has elapsed.

Stand the meat, covered, for the recommended time. Check for correct standing temperature.

Roasting times

For well-done roast beef, cook on MEDIUM for 15-18 minutes per 500 g. Allow to stand for 15 minutes.

For medium roast beef, cook on MEDIUM for 12-14 minutes per 500 g. Allow to stand for 15 minutes.

For rare roast beef, cook on MEDIUM for 10-12 minutes per 500 g. Allow to stand for 15 minutes.

Roast lamb should be cooked on HIGH for 10 minutes per 500 g, then on MEDIUM HIGH for 10 minutes per 500 g. Allow to stand for 15 minutes.

Roast pork should be cooked on MEDIUM for 14-16 minutes per 500 g. Allow to stand for 15-20 minutes.

A veal roast with a bone weighing about 500 g should be cooked on MEDIUM for 18-20 minutes and allowed to stand for 15 minutes.

A boned and rolled veal joint (about 500 g) should be cooked on HIGH for 9-10 minutes. Allow to stand for 15 minutes.

Salt
Do not season meat with salt before cooking as salt will draw out the juices and make the meat tough.

Sausages
The colour of microwaved sausages can be improved by using a browning dish or by basting with equal quantities of soy sauce and honey, or brushing with diluted gravy browning before cooking.

Always prick sausages all over with a fork to prevent bursting.

Sausages should be cooked on HIGH. Take care not to overcook them, or they will be dry and hard. Allow about 1 minute per sausage cooking time.

The fat content will affect the cooking time of sausages.

Stewing
See Casseroling

Stir-frying
Trim meat of any fat, and cut into very thin strips across the grain. Preheat a casserole browning dish on HIGH for 8 minutes. Quickly add 2 teaspoons oil, meat, onion wedges, garlic and ginger. Stir well. (The heat of the browning dish should be sufficient to cook the meat.)

Add enough stir-fry sauce to moisten the ingredients.

If meat needs extra cooking, return it to the oven on MEDIUM for 2-3 minutes.

Thermometer
If using a meat thermometer, ensure that it is inserted into the thickest part of the joint and does not touch the bone in the meat.

POULTRY

Cooking poultry in a microwave oven has much in common with other types of food, especially meat. Roasting bags are useful as a way of preventing splattering, but they should not be secured with metal ties as these cause arcing. Boned and rolled poultry cooks more evenly because the shape and thickness are consistent. Portions of poultry should be arranged so that the thinnest parts point towards the centre of the dish and should be turned during cooking to ensure even penetration by microwaves. Salt toughens poultry if added before cooking and should therefore be added after cooking.

Poultry also tends not to brown in microwave cooking but there are many ways in which colour (and extra flavour) can be added by using bastes. Several such hints are given here.

Whole chickens can be roasted in a microwave oven. Even easier, however, are chicken pieces, which can be quickly prepared for recipes requiring cooked chicken. Chicken stock for soups is another fast, nutritious and tasty microwave speciality.

Boneless chicken breasts

Boneless chicken breasts can be cooked in a microwave oven for 10 minutes per 500 g on MEDIUM HIGH.

Browning chicken

Because chicken is low in fat content, it won't brown in a microwave oven.

Using a baste is one of the best ways to add colour and it also adds extra flavour.

Patting a chicken dry with paper towels before cooking also helps.

Other alternatives are covering the chicken with a split roasting bag and placing the chicken under a

hot grill for a few minutes after cooking.

Chicken

Because it cooks so quickly and the method of cooking uses moist rather than dry heat, the skin of a microwaved roast chicken will not be very brown or crisp. Even so, microwaved chicken is ideal for salads, sandwiches or recipes for which cooked chicken is required.

Place the chicken, neatly trussed, inside a roasting bag, breast side down, and use a roasting rack. Turn the chicken halfway through cooking. Cook on MEDIUM HIGH, allowing 8-10 minutes per 500 g.

Chicken bastes

Chicken can be brushed with any of the following mixtures to give it colour: equal quantities of lemon and honey; equal quantities of honey, brown sugar and soy sauce; melted butter and a pinch of paprika; 2 tablespoons soy sauce, 2 tablespoons sherry and 1 teaspoon freshly grated ginger; 2 tablespoons tomato sauce and 1 tablespoon soy sauce.

Chicken pieces can be dipped in breadcrumbs or coating mixes.

Chicken can be brushed with jellies, preserves, glazes or marmalades halfway through the cooking time.

Soy, teriyaki and barbecue sauces can all be brushed over chicken. Other ideas are onion soup and gravy mix.

Small quantities of dried herbs or spices mixed with melted unsalted butter or oil give additional colour to poultry.

Chicken drumsticks

For even cooking, choose chicken drumsticks of about the same size.

Chicken pieces

Chicken pieces should be positioned skin side up with thinner parts towards the centre and repositioned halfway through cooking time. Allow 8-10 minutes per 500 g on MEDIUM HIGH. Allow to stand for 5-10 minutes.

Chicken skin

Whole chickens can be cooked without their skin, which is ideal for people who are trying to lose weight. If you remove the skin, reduce the cooking time.

Chicken stock

Remove the skin from 350 g chicken necks and backs and hit the bones lightly with a hammer to break them up.

Place them in a large casserole dish and add 3 chopped celery stalks with leaves, 3 chopped carrots, a handful of fresh parsley, 1 chopped onion, 2 chopped spring onions, 1 chopped, dried mushroom, ½ cup dry white wine, 7 black peppercorns and 3½ cups water.

Cover tightly and microwave on HIGH for about 20 minutes, stirring or shaking halfway through. Allow to stand for 20 minutes, then strain. Refrigerate overnight.

For variations on chicken stock, instead of parsley use fresh tarragon, rosemary or sage; add 3 slices of fresh ginger; add 3 fresh hot chilli peppers; or use leek instead of onion.

Cooking time

You can use the size and weight of a chicken as a guide to its cooking time. For a size 11 or 1.1 kg bird, cook for 11 minutes on each side on MEDIUM HIGH; for a size 13 or 1.3 kg bird, cook for 13 minutes.

Defatting duck

Use poultry shears to cut a 2.5 kg duck to pieces, or ask the butcher to do it for you. Discard the back and wings, and trim off all excess fat.

Place the pieces in a drainer with a bottom container to catch the fat. Cover and microwave on HIGH for 7-10 minutes.

Allow to stand for 5 minutes so that the fat can continue to drip, then marinate or roast the meat.

Duck

Duck can be roasted whole in a microwave oven. Cook on MEDIUM, allowing 7-9 minutes per 500 g. Turn halfway through cooking time and allow to stand after cooking for 10-15 minutes.

When cooking duck, spoon off the fat during cooking to prevent a pool forming and splattering occurring, and cover with a split roasting bag.

Duck portions

Duck portions should be placed with the skin side up

and thinner parts towards the centre of the oven. Turn the pieces halfway through cooking.

Four pieces of about 300 g each should be cooked for 10 minutes on HIGH, then 30-35 minutes on MEDIUM.

Goose
Goose should be cooked on MEDIUM HIGH for 12 minutes per 500 g.

Kebabs
Use wooden skewers for chicken kebabs. (Metal skewers will cause arcing.) The meat should preferably be marinated.

Recipe conversion
Your favourite glazes and crumb coatings can be used for microwaved poultry without any changes in ingredients. Stuffing should be a little drier. *See* Stuffing (below).

Sauté vegetables and sausage for stuffings in the microwave mixing bowl to save preparation and clean up time.

Roasting poultry
Compact food cooks more evenly in a microwave oven, so tuck wings underneath and tie legs together with an elastic band or string before roasting.

Always roast poultry elevated on a roasting rack

or inverted saucer in a microwave baking dish.

Shield wings and legs with foil to prevent overcooking.

Begin cooking with the breast side down and turn halfway through cooking.

Cover with paper towel or a split oven bag to stop splattering during cooking. This will also help to crisp the poultry.

After cooking, cover the bird with foil to keep it warm while you cook the rest of the meal.

Simple chicken
Take 500 g chicken fillets and trim off all excess fat. Pound them to achieve an even thickness.

Arrange the fillets in a microwave-safe ring pan (to help the chicken cook evenly) and sprinkle with lemon or lime juice, dry white wine or a herb.

Cover with cling film, pierce the top and microwave on MEDIUM HIGH until cooked through — about 8-10 minutes. Allow to stand for several minutes.

Use in any recipe requiring cooked chicken, serve with mustards or chutneys, keep for use in chicken sandwiches or use in a chicken salad.

Stuffing
If you have stuffed a chicken, you will need to

add about 2 minutes extra cooking time.

When making up your usual stuffing keep the mixture a little drier than usual. Leave out eggs and only use a little milk or butter to moisten the mixture if necessary.

Tender poultry

Smaller pieces of poultry will be more tender than larger ones after microwave cooking.

Therefore a large bird, such as a turkey, might be better cooked in a conventional oven.

Pounding chicken fillets so that they are of equal thickness will help them microwave evenly. Try placing the fillets between two sheets of waxed paper and pound them with the bottom of a sauté pan.

Turkey

Turkey should be cooked on MEDIUM for 15-18 minutes per 500 g weight. Turn three or four times during cooking, depending on size. Start cooking with the breast side down. Allow to stand after cooking for 10-15 minutes.

Use a special microwave thermometer and make sure that the internal temperature remains 77°C for 30 minutes after removing the bird from the oven.

FISH

One of the great characteristics of microwave ovens is the way they cook fish. The speed of cooking ensures firm, moist flesh without the loss of its delicate flavour or any nutritional value. However, timing is critical because overcooking destroys the flavour and makes the flesh tough. Always cook for the minimum time given in a recipe, then check.

Fish should always be cooked in a flat dish. Thinner parts can be overlapped but thicker parts should not be. Fish does not retain its heat for long after leaving the oven, so the order of cooking a meal must be organised so that fish is not left standing for long. If a recipe includes hard vegetables always precook them before the fish. Fish should be white through and flake easily when cooked.

Do not attempt to cook scallops in their shells or oysters, live crayfish or live crabs in the microwave oven. You can, however, use a microwave to open oyster shells.

Arrangement

Arrange small whole fish in a cartwheel, their tails towards the centre, for even cooking.

Boil-in-the-bag fish

Boil-in-the-bag fish can be microwaved in their bags. Pierce the bags before cooking.

Brown paper packages

Fish can be microwaved in brown paper, either bags or wrapped as packages.

This is a good idea when you are cooking fish with plenty of natural moisture or which still have their skins on.

Take a 50-cm piece of brown paper (or a paper bag), which will be large enough for 500 g fish. Place the fish, skin side down (if it has skin), on half the paper, rub the flesh with spices, herbs or mustard and sprinkle with sliced vegetables. Then fold the paper over and crimp the edges closed.

A paper bag should be folded over with the open end tucked underneath.

You don't need to rub the paper with oil. Put the package on a plate and cook on MEDIUM for about 6 minutes.

There might be liquid at the bottom of the package

when you open it so take
care when lifting the fish on
to a serving plate.

Bursting

When cooking whole fish,
slash their skins in two or
three places on both sides
to prevent them bursting
while cooking.

Cooking time

Fish cooks very quickly
and care must be taken to
ensure that it does not
overcook.

Remember that standing
time is part of cooking
time, as heat equalises
throughout the food during
standing time.

Fish fillets or cutlets should
be cooked on MEDIUM
for 6-8 minutes per
500 g.

Whole fish should be
cooked on HIGH
for 5 minutes per
500 g.

Whole crayfish should
be cooked on HIGH
for 10-12 minutes per
500 g.

Mussels should be cooked
on MEDIUM HIGH
for 6-8 minutes per
500 g.

Whole octopus should be
cooked on MEDIUM
for 12-15 minutes per
500 g.

Peeled prawns should
be cooked on MEDIUM
for 3-4 minutes per
500 g.

Scallops should be cooked
on MEDIUM HIGH
for 4-5 minutes per
500 g.

Squid rings should be
cooked on MEDIUM
for 4-5 minutes per
500 g.

Covering fish
Unless instructions are
given to the contrary,
always cover fish when
microwaving.

A cover could equally be
the lid of a dish or cling
film.

A sauce or crusty topping
over the fish is also a
cover.

Crab
To microwave king crab
legs, place 4 legs (about
250 g each) in a bamboo
steamer. Sprinkle with
lemon juice and put a
lemon slice on the exposed
snowy white flesh of the
shoulder. Cover the
steamer and put it on a
plate to catch the drips.
Cook on MEDIUM HIGH
for 7-8 minutes, rotating
the legs about halfway.
Allow to stand for 3
minutes before serving.

Crab claws can be cooked
in the same manner except
that claws should be

arranged in a ring around the edge of the bamboo steamer with the pinchers facing in.

Sixteen claws will take 3-3½ minutes on HIGH.

Doneness
Test fish for doneness by flaking with a fork.

Mussels are cooked when the shells open partially.

Oysters curl at the edges when done, and other seafood turns from translucent to opaque.

Do not overcook fish or seafood, which is delicate and may dry out or toughen.

Check for doneness after the minimum time and let it stand to complete cooking when the recipe directs it.

Do not ...
... cook scallops in their shells, oysters, live crayfish or whole crab in the microwave oven.

All these types of fish must be cooked conventionally.

Drying
Brush the skin of fish with melted butter or margarine to prevent drying out during cooking.

Even cooking
Before cooking a fillet of fish check to see that it is

of even thickness. If not —
and most fillets are not
— tuck the thinner ends
under the middle so that
the whole fillet will cook
evenly.

Fillets
Fillets of fish may be
cooked flat or rolled up,
and should be repositioned
during cooking.

When cooking fish fillets
flat, overlap thin parts to
prevent overcooking of the
thinner parts.

Health
The speed of microwave
cooking leaves fish moist
and succulent without
adding fat and calories.

Fatty acids found in fish
can help to lower your
cholesterol level, and
fish cooks well in a microwave.

Kebabs
When microwaving fish
kebabs use wooden skewers
as metal ones will cause
arcing.

Large fish
Large fish should be
cooked in a single layer
and turned over once
during cooking.

Oven bag fish
Oven bags are excellent for
microwave-cooking fish
that need plenty of
moisture.

Shake about 1 tablespoon flour around in the bag, then add about 500 g fish and about 1 cup/250 ml chopped fresh vegetables and herbs.

Tie a knot in the top of the bag (don't use metal ties) and poke half a dozen slits in the bag with the point of a sharp knife.

Put the bag on a plate and cook on MEDIUM for about 5-6 minutes, rotating the bag halfway through.

The liquid that forms at the bottom of the bag during cooking can, of course, be used as a sauce.

Oyster shells

Place 6 oysters in shells around the turntable and cook on HIGH for 30 seconds. The shells will then pop open.

Paper towels

Avoid microwaving fish on paper towels because it can stick and be difficult to remove.

Instead, place the fish directly on a plate or in a dish and drain before serving or saucing.

Prawns

Peel prawns before microwaving. The shells tend to stick to the flesh and are often difficult to remove.

If you don't want the peeled prawns to curl during microwaving, skewer them with toothpicks.

Smaller prawns take less time to microwave than larger ones.

Recipe conversion

If your recipe calls for poaching fish and then making a sauce with the stock, use only as much liquid as you will need for the sauce.

When fish or seafood are cooked in a sauce, microwave the sauce first. Add fish or seafood towards the end of micro-waving when they are combined with long-cooking ingredients.

Casseroles calling for cooked or canned ingredients will be done when heated through.

When preparing uncooked fish or seafood, use a microwave recipe as a guide to time, and check frequently to avoid overcooking.

Loaves made with canned salmon or tuna usually need no change in ingredients.

Use MEDIUM HIGH unless the sauce is enriched with cream or eggs, which require a setting of MEDIUM or lower.

Stir seafood and casseroles when possible to speed cooking and help distribute heat.

Salt
Salt added before microwave cooking will toughen and dry out the fish during cooking, so add salt after cooking.

Sashimi
Sashimi (pickled ginger) is an excellent accompaniment to cold poached fish and can be stored in the refrigerator for up to a week.

Combine 2 tablespoons finely minced fresh ginger, 1 tablespoon rice vinegar, $1/2$ teaspoon honey and a pinch of ground ginger in a small bowl.

Cover with cling film, pierce the top of it and cook on full power for $1^{1}/2$ minutes. Chill before serving.

Steaks
When cooking fish steaks, arrange them with the thinner ends facing in towards the centre of the container.

Stock
Combine the shells of 500 g prawns (rinsed), 3 cups water, $1/2$ cup dry white

wine, $1/4$ chopped lemon including skin, 1 chopped carrot, 1 chopped onion, 1 chopped celery stalk, 3 bay leaves, 5 black peppercorns and 1 sprig fresh parsley.

Cook in the microwave on HIGH for about 15 minutes and allow to stand for about 15 minutes.

Strain before using.

FRUIT AND
VEGETABLES

FRUIT AND
 VEGETABLES

Fruit cooked in a microwave oven keeps its shape better and looks more attractive than fruit cooked conventionally. If a recipe requires a soft purée, just cook the fruits a few minutes longer.

Fruit with a firm skin, such as apples, needs to be scored or pierced so that it does not burst during cooking. Whole firm fruit, such as apricots, cherries, peaches, nectarines and pears, is delicious when poached in a sugar syrup. Peaches, apricots and nectarines do not need skinning before microwaving because the skin peels away easily after cooking.

Most vegetables microwave very successfully. Because they are cooked quickly they retain their colour, flavour and nutrients well. For the best results use fresh vegetables and cut them into uniform-sized pieces so that they are cooked evenly. Frozen vegetables need only a very small amount of water. Always pierce whole vegetables with skins to prevent them from bursting.

Apples

Peel, core and slice, then cover and cook on HIGH allowing 3-4 minutes for 250 g and 5-6 minutes for 500 g. Allow to stand for 3 minutes.

To make apple purée, cook for a further 3 minutes with 1 tablespoon water until the apple slices are soft and collapsed, then mash until smooth.

See also Baked apple

Apricots

Wash and dry the fruit and remove any stalks, and when cooking whole pierce the skins before poaching in syrup.

Apricots may also be stoned and halved before cooking.

Add the apricots to syrup, cover and cook 500 g fruit on HIGH for 4-5 minutes and stir halfway through cooking.

Alternatively, add 15 ml apple juice or water to the apricots and cook as above. Allow to stand for 3 minutes.

Artichokes (globe)

Trim the stem ends so that the artichokes will stand up straight, then use scissors to cut off the leaf tips.

Wrap each one in a damp paper towel or place in a

dish with 1 tablespoon water and cover.

Allow 4-5 minutes on HIGH for 1 globe, 6-8 minutes for 2 globes and 10-12 minutes for 4 globes.

Artichokes (jerusalem)
Peel and cut off knobs. Slice thickly and place in a dish with 2 tablespoons water.

Cook and microwave on HIGH for 5-6 minutes (for 250 g) and 8-9 minutes for 500 g. Allow to stand for 3 minutes.

Asparagus
Asparagus should be arranged on a plate like the spokes of a wheel, with the stalks towards the outside of the dish.

Cook fresh asparagus on HIGH allowing 3-4 minutes per 500 g.

Frozen asparagus should be cooked on HIGH for 4-5 minutes per 500 g quantity.

Avocados
Firm avocados can be ripened by microwaving them on MEDIUM HIGH for 2-3 minutes.

Baked apple
For an excellent quick breakfast, snack or dessert, take a cooking apple, remove the core, wrap the apple in cling film and poke

with a skewer a dozen
times.

Microwave on HIGH until
tender — about 3 minutes.

Then, using rubber gloves,
remove the cling film,
fill the core with grated
cheddar, minced raisins
and walnuts, and allow to
stand for 2 minutes.

Bananas
Peel and cut firm bananas
into slices, then place in a
dish.

Sprinkle with a little lemon
juice and 1 teaspoon brown
sugar per banana.

Cover and cook on HIGH,
allowing 2-3 minutes for

2 bananas and 3-4 minutes
for 4 bananas. Stand for
2 minutes.

Beans, dry *See* Pulses

Beans, green
To achieve the best colour
and texture, green beans
should be cut into pieces
before microwaving.

One-centimetre pieces
work well. Young, tender
green beans will give you
the best results.

Place 500 g rinsed, still
wet, green bean pieces in a
dish, cover and microwave
on HIGH for about $4^1/_2$
minutes. Allow to stand for
3 minutes before serving.

Whole frozen green beans should be cooked on HIGH for 6-8 minutes per 500 g.

Beetroot
Beetroot should be pierced several times and cooked uncovered. For 4 medium-sized beetroot, allow 12-14 minutes on HIGH.

Blackberries
Place 500 g blackberries in a dish, sprinkle with 75 g sugar and cover, cook on HIGH for 4-6 minutes, stir halfway through cooking and allow to stand for 3 minutes.

Blanching
Small quantities of vegetables blanch more evenly than large — if necessary blanch in batches, microwaving the first batch while preparing the next batch.

A 2-litre casserole dish is suitable for most vegetables.

Broad beans
Fresh broad beans should be cooked in a freezer bag with 1 tablespoon water. Allow 5-6 minutes cooking time on HIGH per 500 g.

Frozen broad beans should be cooked on HIGH for 7-8 minutes per 500 g.

Broccoli
Place fresh broccoli in a freezer bag and cook on

HIGH for 3-4 minutes per 500 g.

Frozen broccoli should be cooked on HIGH for 6-7 minutes per 500 g.

Chopped broccoli that contains some stalk will take a bit longer to cook than just broccoli florets, especially if the stalk is tough.

Peeling the stalk before chopping cuts the cooking time and helps the florets and stalks to cook more evenly together.

Whole spears of broccoli with florets attached should be arranged, while still wet, on a flat plate like the spokes of a wheel with the florets at the centre to protect their more delicate texture from overcooking.

Cover with cling film.

A 500 g quantity will take about 5 minutes to microwave on HIGH and should be rotated halfway through cooking time. Then allow to stand for about 3 minutes before serving.

Brussels sprouts

When cooking fresh brussels sprouts cut a cross in the base of each sprout and cover the dish. Cook on HIGH for 5-6 minutes per 500 g.

Frozen brussels sprouts should be cooked on HIGH for 6-7 minutes per 500 g.

Cabbage
Half a cabbage, shredded, should be covered and cooked on HIGH for 7-8 minutes (or for 4-5 minutes per 500 g).

Cabbage leaves
Remove the core from a head of cabbage, pull away any ugly outer leaves and then remove 4 nice ones. Rinse them but don't dry them. Stack the leaves together and wrap in cling film.

Microwave on HIGH until the leaves are tender but still crisp — 3-4 minutes.

Allow to stand for 5 minutes before serving or stuffing.

Capsicum
Remove the seeds of a capsicum and cook, whole or sliced, covered, on HIGH for 5-6 minutes per 500 g.

Carrots
Fresh carrots should be cooked, covered, on HIGH for 5-6 minutes per 500 g.

Frozen carrots should be cooked on HIGH for 6-7 minutes per 500 g.

Carrots can easily be cooked in wet paper towels. Simply stack three towels together and wet them with water.

Squeeze out slightly, then lay them out flat.

Set 250 g thinly sliced carrot rounds in the centre of the towels, sprinkle with dill and close up the towels like an envelope.

Place the package on a plate and cook on HIGH for about 4 minutes, rotating once during cooking. Allow to stand for about 3 minutes before serving.

Cauliflower

Half a head of fresh cauliflower, cut into florets and covered, should be cooked on HIGH for 4-5 minutes.

A 500 g quantity of frozen cauliflower florets should be cooked on HIGH for 6-7 minutes.

Celery

Trim and cut 500 g celery stalks into 5 cm lengths. Place in a dish, add 4 tablespoons water and cover.

Cook on HIGH for 6-7 minutes, stirring halfway through. Stand for 3 minutes, drain and serve.

Cherries

Remove stones and place 500 g cherries in a dish with 50-100 g sugar and cover.

Cook on HIGH for 3-4 minutes and allow to stand for 3 minutes.

Chutneys *See* Preserves

Citrus fruits

If there is a limp, almost lifeless half lemon, lime or orange in your fridge, place it face down on a damp paper towel and microwave it on HIGH for about 20 seconds. Then use it for juice or slice it.

Coconuts

To prepare a coconut for eating, find the softest of its three eyes, then pierce it with a screwdriver and hit it with a hammer. Keep hitting until the eye is punctured and the coconut just beings to crack.

Then drain the juice and reserve it. Wrap the coconut in cling film and microwave on HIGH until fragrant and very hot, which takes about 5 minutes.

Let it stand for 15 minutes, then hit it hard with a hammer until it splits.

Remove the meat with a strong knife and store it, tightly covered, in the refrigerator.

Corn kernels

Frozen corn kernels should be cooked on HIGH for 3-4 minutes per 250 g.

Corn on the cob

Pull the husk over the corn or cover it with cling film. Cook 1 fresh cob on HIGH for 3 minutes, 2 cobs for 6 minutes and 4 cobs for 10 minutes.

Frozen whole corn cobs should be cooked on HIGH for 3-4 minutes for 1 cob, 6-7 minutes for 2 cobs and 8-10 minutes for 4 cobs.

Covering
Always cover the container when microwaving vegetables unless instructions are given to the contrary.

Wrap large vegetables without skins in cling film or cook in a covered casserole.

Cracked wheat
Combine 1 cup coarse cracked wheat, 1½ cups water and 1 bay leaf in a 23-cm glass pie dish, cover with cling film and pierce the top.

Microwave on HIGH until the wheat is tender — about 5-6 minutes.

Allow to stand for 5 minutes. Remove the bay leaf and drain excess water (if necessary) before serving.

Dates
Place 250 g dried dates in a dish and pour 150 ml boiling water over them.

Cover the dish and cook for 3-4 minutes on HIGH, stirring once. Leave to stand for 10-15 minutes.

Dried fruit
To plump up dried fruit, place it in a bowl, cover with water, milkless tea or fruit juice and cook on

HIGH for 5 minutes. Stir, leave to stand for 5 minutes and drain well.

Instead of soaking dried fruit overnight, put the fruit in a bowl with soaking liquid (e.g. fruit juice), cover and microwave on HIGH for 2-5 minutes.

Stir the fruit thoroughly and, if it is still cold, cook for a further 2 minutes or until just warm.

Allow to cool before using in a cake recipe.

Eggplant

A 500 g eggplant, sliced and placed in a covered dish with 1 tablespoon butter, should be cooked on HIGH for 5-6 minutes.

Grapefruit

Cut a grapefruit in half and slice between the membrane of each segment (using a special-purpose grapefruit knife) to release them from the pith.

Sprinkle with brown sugar if desired, place in a shallow dish and cook on HIGH for 2 minutes, turning the fruit around halfway through cooking. Serve hot.

Herbs

To dry herbs, strip the leaves off the stems and arrange them in a single layer on a piece of absorbent kitchen paper. Cook on HIGH for 1 minute. Turn the leaves over, reposition them and cook for a further 1-1½ minutes until dry.

Jams

A microwave oven is particularly useful for making jams and preserves when you only have a small quantity of fruit.

Always use a large bowl to prevent the liquid from boiling over.

Use a container made of a material that withstands the high temperature of boiling sugar.

To warm sugar for jam-making, place the sugar in a 2-litre dish and cook on HIGH for 1-1½ minutes.

The skins of citrus fruits such as lemon, orange and grapefruit tend to remain firm when cooked.

For more tender skins, grate or chop the rind finely before using.

Use the same proportion of fruit, sugar and pectin.

Paraffin wax for sealing jars must be melted conventionally; it will not melt in the microwave oven because it is transparent to microwave energy.

See also Preserves

Kebabs

Mushroom caps, pearl onions, zucchini chunks and eggplant cubes make excellent microwave kebabs.

Choose vegetables with similar textures and sizes and marinate them before cooking.

Thread the vegetables on a 15-cm bamboo skewer and place them around the rim of a large flat plate.

Cover with cling film (pierce it) and microwave on HIGH for 4-4½ minutes per 500 g vegetables.

The skewers must be rotated halfway through cooking time.

Allow to stand for about 3 minutes before serving.

Kohlrabi

Use kohlrabis no more than about 7 cm in diameter.

To microwave 500 g, snip off the roots and stems, then cut into quarters.

Place the quarters in a 23-cm dish and add 3 tablespoons chicken stock.

Cover with cling film, vent the top and cook on HIGH for about 7 minutes, stirring or shaking every 2 minutes.

Allow to stand for about 5 minutes, or until cooked enough to handle.

To peel, slip a paring knife between the skin and flesh

and pull down. The skin will come off easily.

Leeks
Leeks should be covered and cooked on HIGH for 3-4 minutes per 500 g.

Liquid
When microwave-cooking vegetables, use a minimum of water. Some vegetables cook in their own natural moisture. Two tablespoons to $1/4$ cup liquid is usually enough for others.

Mixed vegetables
A 250 g quantity of frozen mixed vegetables should be cooked on HIGH for 5-6 minutes.

Mushrooms
Wipe with a damp cloth and trim off the stalks. Place 100 g mushrooms in a bowl and dot with butter.

Cook on HIGH for $1^{1}/_{2}$-2 minutes, stirring once during cooking. Stand for 1 minute.

To rehydrate dried mushrooms in the microwave, remove stems from 4 mushrooms, rinse and place in a large bowl.

Pour in enough water to cover the mushrooms, cover the top with cling film, pierce it and cook on HIGH for about 5 minutes. Allow to stand for another 5 minutes.

Nectarines
Place 250 g nectarines in a dish and add 600 ml syrup or fruit juice. Cover and cook on HIGH for 2-3 minutes, stirring once during cooking. Stand for 3 minutes.

Nuts
To roast nuts, spread 100 g shelled nuts on a plate and cook, uncovered on HIGH for 2-3 minutes until lightly browned, stirring 2-3 times.

Allow a little longer for whole nuts than for chopped nuts.

Onions
Fresh, sliced onions should be covered and cooked on HIGH for 5-6 minutes per 500 g.

Whole small or sliced frozen onions should be cooked on HIGH for 2-3 minutes per 100 g.

Many recipes require sautéed onions. Microwave them instead and avoid adding extra fat to your cooking. Place 2 tablespoons finely chopped onions in a small dish, cover with cling film and pierce the top. Cook on HIGH until tender — about 1½ minutes.

Parsnips
Place 500 g washed, trimmed and peeled parsnips in a dish with 2 tablespoons water, 1 teaspoon lemon juice and a knob of butter.

Cover and cook for 8-10 minutes. Rearrange halfway through cooking time. Allow to stand for 2-3 minutes, drain and add more butter before serving.

Peaches
Place 250 g peeled peaches in a dish and add 600 ml syrup or fruit juice. Cover and cook on HIGH for 2-3 minutes, stirring once. Stand for 3 minutes.

Pears
Pour 300 ml cider or red wine into a dish, add 100 g sugar and cook on HIGH for 5 minutes, stirring once. Arrange pears (peeled and cut lengthwise) in the syrup with the narrow ends towards the centre. Cook

on HIGH, allowing 3-4 minutes for 250 g and 5-7 minutes for 500 g, turning halfway through cooking. Allow to cool in the syrup.

Peas
Fresh peas should be covered and cooked on HIGH for 4-5 minutes per 500 g.

Frozen peas should also be covered and cooked on HIGH for 5-6 minutes per 500 g.

A mixture of frozen peas and carrots should be cooked on HIGH for 6-7 minutes per 500 g.

Plums
Halve the fruit and remove the stones. Place in a dish

with a little sugar and 2 tablespoons water or red wine. Cover the dish and cook 250 g plums on HIGH for 3 minutes and 500 g for 5 minutes. Stir once during cooking. Allow to stand for 5 minutes.

Potatoes
Excellent results are obtained when micro-waving jacket potatoes. Pierce the skins with a fork, place on the turntable and cook 2 medium or 4 small potatoes for 4-5 minutes on HIGH. Leave to stand for 5 minutes wrapped in foil.

To make mashed potatoes, or to prepare potato for potato salad, peel, cube and rinse potatoes and place in a freezer bag. Cook on HIGH, allowing 8-10 minutes per 500 g.

Preserves
Fruits and vegetables for preserves should be finely chopped, then cooked with sugar, vinegar and flavouring ingredients to a thick sauce with no excess liquid.

Stir regularly in order to redistribute the sugar in the mixture so that it cooks evenly.

Cook chutneys until there is no pool of liquid on the surface and the mixture is thick.

Pickles, chutney and relishes need to mature for at least two months before eating.

See also Jams

Pulses

Some pulses (aduki beans, black-eye beans, chickpeas, flageolet beans, mung beans and split peas or lentils) will microwave successfully and quickly.

However, pulses with very tough skins (red kidney beans, black beans, butter beans, cannellini beans, haricot beans and soya beans) will not cook in less time and are better cooked conventionally, as are large quantities of pulses.

To cook pulses, soak the beans overnight, then drain and cover with enough boiling water to come about 2.5 cm above the level of the beans. Cover and cook on HIGH for 25-35 minutes (aduki beans, black-eye beans, mung beans and split peas or lentils), 40-45 minutes (for flageolet beans) or 50-55 minutes (for chickpeas).

Allow to stand for 5 minutes after cooking. Do not drain.

If there is no time to soak pulses or dry beans overnight, place them in a large casserole dish and cover with water. Microwave on HIGH until boiling, then simmer for 30 minutes on MEDIUM LOW or DEFROST. Stand covered for 15-20 minutes, then drain, rinse and cook.

Pumpkin

Small pumpkins can be cooked whole in their shells; larger pumpkins should be sliced or cubed and cooked covered.

A 500 g quantity needs to cook for 8-10 minutes on HIGH.

If you have a pumpkin or squash that's hard to cut, wrap it in waxed paper and microwave it. A 500 g vegetable cooked on HIGH needs about 2 minutes, then it will be much easier to cut.

Recipe conversion

When converting vegetable recipes, reduce the liquid from your conventional recipe to the amount needed for microwaving (see the hints in this chapter for specific vegetables). Remember that time depends on amount as well as type of vegetable.

With vegetable combinations, add quick-cooking ingredients towards the end of microwaving.

Precook the fillings for stuffed vegetables, then microwave the stuffed vegetables for the same amount of time as a whole one. Partially cook large, dense vegetables, like squash, before stuffing.

Rhubarb
Place 500 g rhubarb (washed, trimmed and cut into 2-5 cm lengths) in a dish with 3 tablespoons water. Cover and cook on HIGH for 7-8 minutes, stirring twice. Then stir in 100 g sugar towards the end of the cooking time. Allow to stand for 3 minutes.

Roasting vegetables
When cooking a roast meal in a hurry, precook prepared vegetables in the microwave oven, then finish the cooking process in a frypan or under a grill to make them crisp and brown.

To precook the vegetables, place them in a covered container and microwave on HIGH until almost tender.

Salt
When cooking vegetables in the microwave oven the flavour is retained and salt is usually not necessary.

If you do want to add salt, mix it with water first.

Once salt is dissolved it will not make the vegetables dry out.

Spinach

Add 1 tablespoon water to fresh spinach and cook, covered, on HIGH for 3-5 minutes per 250 g.

Frozen spinach, leaf or chopped, should be cooked on HIGH for 6-7 minutes per 250 g.

Spinach for stuffing

Use fresh spinach rather than frozen — it's more nutritious.

Mince 2 cups (about 500 ml) packed leaves in a food processor, then place then in a 23-cm pie dish, cover with cling film, pierce the top and cook on HIGH for about 1 minute. Allow to

stand for 1 minute before draining.

The result will be about 100 ml spinach, which can be used in fish or chicken stuffings.

Standing time

Standing time is important, especially with large, whole vegetables. It allows the centre to tenderise without overcooking the outside.

During standing time, keep the food covered to hold in heat. Long standing times can be used to microwave other foods.

Sweet potatoes

Peel, slice and cook sweet potatoes on HIGH for 8-10 minutes per 500 g.

Tomatoes

Pierce whole tomatoes and cover sliced or cubed tomatoes. Cook on HIGH for 5-6 minutes per 500 g.

To microwave dried tomatoes, place four in a little bowl with enough chicken stock to cover them. Cover with cling film and cook on HIGH for 1½-2 minutes, depending on size. Allow to stand until cool enough to handle.

To peel a tomato with the microwave, carve an X in the skin of the stem end. Then wrap the tomato in a paper towel and microwave for 1 minute. Small, ripe tomatoes will take less time than large, underripe ones.

Allow to stand until cool enough to handle, then peel off the skin with a paring knife.

Turnips

Wash turnips, peel and chop larger ones into segments, slices or chunks; leave smaller ones whole.

Place 500 g prepared turnip in a dish with 3 tablespoons water. Cover and cook on HIGH for 8-10 minutes until tender, stirring twice. Allow to stand for 2 minutes, then drain well.

Frozen turnip should be cooked on HIGH for 6-7 minutes per 250 g.

Vegetables

Always place the stems of vegetables like cauliflower or broccoli towards the outside of the dish. The stems are tougher than the flower, so this will ensure even cooking.

Always stir vegetables or rearrange them halfway through cooking.

When cooking whole vegetables, such as potatoes in their skins, arrange them in a circle with a space between each one. Don't put one in the centre.

Most vegetables tend to have a crisp texture when cooked.

If very soft vegetables are required, use the conventional method of cooking.

Frozen vegetables can be cooked without being defrosted first and need no added liquid.

Fresh vegetables require a small amount of water to create steam for cooking.

Small frozen vegetables such as peas, sweetcorn kernels and mixed vegetables can be cooked in their plastic packets because the melting ice within the packet produces enough moisture for cooking. Split the top of the packet and shake it about halfway through the cooking to distribute the heat evenly.

Walnuts

To shell 1 cup walnuts or pecans, place in a 23-cm glass pie dish with 3 tablespoons water.

Cover and microwave on HIGH for about 2 minutes. Then drain and allow to stand until cool enough to handle, then shell.

Zucchini

A whole fresh zucchini should be pierced before cooking; a sliced fresh zucchini should be covered.

Cook on HIGH for 5-6 minutes per 500 g.

Frozen sliced zucchini should be cooked on HIGH for 3-4 minutes per 250 g.

SOUPS AND SAUCES

This chapter contains hints, both general and particular, and useful recipes for soups, sauces, savouries, spices and stock.

It also contains hints for successful egg, cheese, pasta and rice cooking.

A microwave oven makes it easy to prepare nutritious soups in a fraction of the usual time and with less fat and salt. Sauces are much easier and quicker to prepare in a microwave oven; so is stock. Spices can be precooked to release their flavour before being added to the main dish without being fried in oil.

Barbecue sauce

This barbecue sauce should be used for basting during the last 5 minutes of grilling.

In a small bowl combine ½ cup tomato purée, ¼ cider vinegar, 1 tablespoon worcestershire sauce, ½ teaspoon hot pepper sauce, 2 cloves garlic (crushed), 1 bay leaf and a pinch of ground ginger.

Cover the bowl with cling film and pierce the top.

Microwave on HIGH until fragrant and just bubbly — about 2 minutes. Allow to stand for about 5 minutes. Remove the bay leaf before serving.

Boiling eggs

Eggs cooked in their shells in a microwave oven are likely to explode due to the build up of internal pressure.

But you can boil them if you know how! Wrap an egg totally in aluminium foil and place the egg in a 1-cup glass jug with ½ cup hot water.

For a soft-boiled egg, cook on HIGH 4-5 minutes and 5-6 minutes for hard-boiled.

Allow to stand in the cooking water for 2 minutes (soft-boiled) and 5 minutes (hard-boiled) before serving.

To boil more than one egg, use a larger dish and more water, and cook a little longer (say an extra 2-4 minutes).

Cheese

Whenever possible, cheese should be added towards the end of microwave cooking rather than at the beginning. If overcooked, cheese becomes tough and rubbery.

Cheese will cook more evenly in a microwave oven if grated rather than diced or sliced.

A microwave can be used for quickly cooking the basic ingredients of cheese-topped dishes. The surface can then be crisped and browned under a conventional grill.

Chilli sauce

In a small dish combine 6 dried chillies (seeds removed), 6 cloves garlic, 1 bay leaf and water or chicken stock to cover.

Cover the dish with cling flim and microwave on HIGH until the chillies are tender — about 10 minutes. Check halfway through and add more liquid if necessary.

Allow to stand for 10 minutes, and remove the bay leaf. Place the chilli mixture in a blender and blend with 1 tablespoon olive oil, 4 tablespoons chicken stock and 2 tablespoons cider vinegar until smooth.

Coconut milk

Combine 1 tablespoon finely grated coconut milk and $\frac{1}{2}$ cup milk or light cream in a small bowl.

Cover with cling film, vent the top and microwave on MEDIUM until fragrant — about $1\frac{1}{2}$ minutes.

Store, tightly covered, in the refrigerator and strain before use.

Cream cheese

To make a low-fat cream cheese, combine 250 ml buttermilk and 250 ml milk in a 2-litre dish.

Cover and cook on HIGH until the whey separates, the curds form a solid mass in the middle and bubbles appear around the edge of the dish — about 4-$4\frac{1}{2}$ minutes.

Don't boil the mixture hard or the curds will become rubbery, and don't stir.

Cover the dish with a paper towel and set aside to become completely cool — about 3 hours.

Don't skimp on this stage or the cheese will be too watery.

Drain the cheese through a strainer lined with a paper towel until all the whey is gone.

Stir well, then store covered and refrigerate for a week.

Crusty toppings

A dish that has a crusty topping should always be cooked uncovered to avoid a soggy result.

Curry powder

Commercial curry powders — like home-ground spice mixtures — should be heated before use, and the usual thing is to fry them in butter or oil.

Using a microwave achieves the same result without fat.

Place 2 teaspoons curry powder in a small glass dish and cook, uncovered, on HIGH until fragrant — about 1 minute.

Allow to stand for another minute before adding to dressings for poultry salads, for instance, or to a cooked sauce in need of extra flavour.

Eggs

In order to prevent eggs from bursting and exploding in a microwave oven, pierce the yolks gently with a fine skewer or the tip of a sharp knife.

Eggs will cook more evenly if they are at room temperature.

Use a lower power level to microwave eggs. Overcooking makes eggs tough and rubbery.

Standing time is important for many egg dishes, even when they can be stirred during cooking, because eggs are very delicate and can overcook from internal heat.

Eggs and bacon

Preheat a microwave browning dish on HIGH for 4-5 minutes, then add 1 teaspoon oil and coat the base. Add 2 rashers bacon, turn, then move to the side of the dish. Break in 2 eggs carefully and pierce the yolk and white. Cook for 2 minutes on MEDIUM HIGH until the whites are just set.

Garlic

The microwave oven allows you to avoid frying garlic before use and thereby introducing more fat into your cooking.

Chop 4 cloves garlic finely and place them in a small bowl with 2 tablespoons chicken stock.

Cover with cling film and cook on HIGH for about 2 minutes, stirring or shaking halfway through.

Then proceed to use as you would fried garlic.

Ghee
See Butter

Gravy
Place 2 tablespoons dripping or pan juices and 1 small, finely chopped onion in a 4-cup jug.

Cook on HIGH for 2 minutes. Add 2 tablespoons flour, 1 tablespoon tomato paste and 1½ cups beef stock.

Stir well and cook on HIGH for 3-4 minutes.

Stir halfway through cooking. Season with salt and pepper.

Herbs
Dried herbs can be substituted for fresh herbs in microwave cooking by reducing the quantity used, because microwaving makes the flavours of herbs stronger.

For example, 1 teaspoon dried parsley equals 1 tablespoon chopped fresh parsley.

To dry herbs in a microwave oven, place a bunch of fresh herbs on a paper towel and microwave on HIGH until dry.

Rub between your hands and store in an airtight jar.

Hoisin marinade

Combine 2 tablespoons hoisin sauce with 2 tablespoons Chinese red vinegar or red wine vinegar in a small bowl. Cover with cling film, pierce the top and cook on HIGH until heated through — about 40 seconds.

Use to marinate mild white fish.

Horseradish cream

In a small bowl mix together ½ cup milk or light cream, 1 teaspoon cornflour and a pinch of cream of tartar.

Place the bowl on a plate (in case the sauce boils over) and microwave, uncovered, until the sauce begins to thicken — 3-3½ minutes. Stir two or three times.

Then mix in 1 tablespoon prepared horseradish and 1 teaspoon finely chopped fresh parsley or chives.

Chill before serving.

Hot bowls and mugs

To preheat bowls and mugs before serving soup in them, rinse 2-4 bowls or mugs in water, shake them and put them in the microwave. Cover with a sheet of cling film and microwave on HIGH until hot, about 2 minutes.

Hot drink

For a hot drink on a cold night, combine equal parts of tomato juice and beef stock. Add a dash of worcestershire sauce or hot pepper sauce and cook on HIGH until warm — about 1-1½ minutes for 1 cup.

Marinade for poultry

This marinade works equally well with rabbit.

Grind 1 teaspoon green peppercorns finely and combine in a small bowl with 2 tablespoons white vinegar. Cover with cling film, vent the top and microwave on HIGH for about 1½ minutes. Watch it to make sure it doesn't boil. Rub the mixture over rabbit or poultry about an hour before grilling.

Mint sauce

Combine ½ cup water, 1 tablespoon sugar, 2 tablespoons brown sugar and 2 tablespoons finely chopped mint in a 1-cup jug. Cook on HIGH for 30-60 seconds. Stir well.

Mustard sauce

In a small bowl whisk together ½ cup buttermilk, 1 teaspoon cornflour and a pinch of cream of tartar. Microwave, uncovered, on HIGH until the mixture begins to thicken — about 1½-2 minutes — stirring a couple of times.

Next, mix in 2 teaspoons Dijon mustard, 1 tablespoon finely chopped parsley or chives and a dash of worcestershire sauce. Chill before serving.

Olive oil

Olive oil improves in flavour when microwaved. It can be tossed with broccoli or zucchine, fresh from the microwave, and served with crushed thyme or basil.

Paprika

Rather than sautéeing paprika to release its flavour and aroma, prepare it in the microwave oven and leave out the oil or butter.

Place ½ teaspoon paprika in a small dish, cover with cling film, vent the top and cook on HIGH for 1 minute, stopping twice to shake the dish.

Pasta

The best way to cook pasta in a microwave is to put it in a large bowl with salt to taste. Pour over enough boiling water to cover the pasta by 2 cm. Stir and cover, then cook on HIGH for 6-8 minutes for 250 g pasta, stirring occasionally.

Remove the pasta from the oven when it is still slightly undercooked, because prolonged cooking will cause it to become soggy, and part of the cooking occurs during the standing time.

Pasta should be covered and left to stand in its cooking liquid for about 5 minutes, depending on the type of pasta shape (allow longer for larger ones). If you are making a sauce, do so during the standing time.

Frozen pasta can be cooked directly from frozen on the HIGH setting unless combined with a sauce which might spoil or curdle.

Once pasta is tossed in a sauce it can be reheated quickly if necessary and will still retain its freshness.

Poaching eggs
Break the required number of eggs into ramekin dishes or teacups. Gently pierce the yolks with a fine skewer or the tip of a sharp knife. Arrange the dishes in a circle in the oven and cook on MEDIUM LOW or DEFROST until the whites are just set.

(Two eggs will take 2 minutes and four eggs will take 3 minutes.)

Leave to stand for 2 minutes.

Popcorn
Take a large bowl with a lid or heavy plate, a tablespoon of vegetable oil and about 75 g of popping

corn. Put the oil in the bowl and cook on HIGH for 1-2 minutes or until hot. Stir in the corn, cover and cook on HIGH for 7 minutes or until the popping stops, shaking the bowl occasionally. Add salt to taste.

Poppadams

Brush each poppadam with a little oil on one side. Then cook, one at a time, on HIGH for 1 minute or until crisp and puffed up all over.

Quiches

Quiches are easy to microwave. Be sure to microwave the pastry shell first.

When adapting a recipe for microwaving, reduce liquid by about a third.

Heat and stir the egg mixture until slightly set before pouring it into the shell. This helps the filling cook smoothly and set quickly.

A quiche should be removed from the oven when set but not dry. It will firm up after standing for 5 minutes.

Recipe conversion: Rice

The easiest and fastest way to convert a main dish or casserole calling for uncooked rice, meat and vegetables is to substitute quick-cooking rice for uncooked long grain rice.

Meats and vegetables microwave so rapidly that they will be overcooked in the time it takes to tenderise raw rice.

To obtain the same number of servings, substitute twice the amount of quick-cooking rice and use the quantity of liquid recommended on the package.

If you prefer to use raw or converted long grain rice, microwave it until almost tender (about 5 minutes on HIGH followed by 10-13 minutes on MEDIUM for 1 cup long grain). Add the

meat towards the end of cooking.

Recipe conversion: Sauces

Most sauce recipes can be converted to microwave cooking without a change in ingredients.

Flour-based sauces are made by stirring flour into melted fat and adding cooking liquid.

For brown sauces, microwave the flour and fat a few minutes to develop colour. Then blend in liquid, using a wire whisk, and microwave until thickened, stirring occasionally.

The power level depends on the type of liquid used.

Cornflour is usually dissolved in cold water before it is combined with hot liquid.

In sweet sauces, dry cornflour and sugar are blended together before liquid is added. Microwave until the sauce is thickened and translucent, stirring halfway through and at the end of cooking.

If your recipe calls for long, slow simmering to reduce the sauce, add a little more flour when microwave cooking, since the liquid will not evaporate in the short microwaving time.

After the sauce has thickened, reduce the power to MEDIUM and microwave for 20-30 minutes to develop flavour.

Microwave sauces made with cream at MEDIUM HIGH and stir frequently. Double-boiler sauces can be cooked at MEDIUM.

Cooking time will depend on the amount and temperature of the ingredients used. The cook-and-look method works well. Once the ingredients are heated, stir the sauce every minute and check the consistency.

Recipe conversion: Soups

When converting soup

recipes for microwave cooking, reduce the amount of liquid by a quarter, since there will be less evaporation. Exceptions are soups made with dried beans, peas or lentils, which absorb moisture as they cook.

Reduce salt and other seasonings by half. Add more to taste after microwaving.

The type of liquid and the main bulky ingredient determines the power level.

When making soup with less tender meat, start it at HIGH, then reduce the power to MEDIUM.

Vegetable soup and soup with tender meat, such as chicken, can be microwaved at HIGH.

Cut dense vegetables like carrots and potatoes in thin slices or small cubes for fast, uniform cooking.

Cut less tender meat, like stewing beef, into 2 cm cubes to that energy can penetrate from all sides.

HIGH is used for liquids like water, stock or tomato juice. Milk-based soups that are stirred during cooking can also be microwaved at HIGH, but should be placed in a deep container to prevent boiling over.

MEDIUM HIGH and MEDIUM are needed for cream, which curdles at high temperatures, and soups which require simmering to develop flavour or tenderise ingredients like stewing beef, uncooked macaroni, dried beans or peas.

See also Cheese, Eggs, Quiches

Rice

When cooking rice in a microwave oven always stop the cooking process when the rice is still just slightly firm and there is a little water left.

Allow to stand covered until ready to serve. This procedure results in fluffy rice. Overcooking will produce a gluey end product.

Rice should always be cooked uncovered in a microwave oven, because it tends to boil over if covered.

Rice appears flat when cooked in a microwave oven, but it can be fluffed up with a fork.

Rice cooked in the microwave is excellent for fried rice recipes.

Rice cooking times

To cook white rice in a microwave oven, allow 2 cups cold water per 1 cup

rice. Cook on HIGH for
12 minutes and leave to
stand for 2 minutes after
cooking.

To cook brown rice, for
1 cup rice, allow 2½ cups
cold water and cook on
HIGH for 25-30 minutes.
Stand for 2 minutes.

Allow 1¾ cups cold water
for 1 cup 'quick' brown
rice and cook on high for
14 minutes. Leave to stand
for 2 minutes.

Saffron sauce
This richly coloured sauce
can be added to a sauce or
dressing, whether made
with yoghurt or based on
stock.

Combine a pinch of
crushed saffron threads
with 2 tablespoons milk in
a small bowl. Cover with
cling film, vent the top and
cook on HIGH for about
1 minute. Allow to stand
for another minute before
using.

Sauces
Always use a container
large enough to prevent the
sauce from boiling over.

Whisk sauces frequently
during cooking to prevent
lumps forming.

When making sauces
thickened with cornflour
or arrowroot, make sure
the thickening agent is
completely dissolved in

cold liquid before adding a hot one.

Sauces thickened with egg are best cooked on LOW since care is needed to prevent them curdling.

Frozen sauces can be reheated straight from the freezer. Transfer to a bowl, then reheat, stirring to break up any frozen lumps.

Scrambled eggs

To cook perfect scrambled eggs, place 1-2 eggs per person, 1 tablespoon milk and 1 teaspoon butter per egg and pepper to taste in a jug or bowl and mix with a fork.

Cook on MEDIUM HIGH, allowing 1-1½ minutes per egg.

Stir during cooking (once for 2 eggs; once or twice for 4 eggs; two-three times for 8 eggs) with a fork.

Soups

Making your own soups enables you to control the salt and fat content.

When microwaving soups, try to cook the solids with a small amount of liquid, then add hot liquid later. This way soups will cook faster and their flavours will be enhanced.

One exception is when making stocks and other

soups that must be microwaved with a large volume of liquid, in which case you need to use a dish twice the volume of what you're cooking to avoid boiling over.

Soup flavour
The flavour of microwaved soups will improve if made in advance, refrigerated for several hours and then reheated.

Sour cream
When adding sour cream to a dish use a lower power level for cooking.

Add the sour cream as late in the process as possible and avoid overcooking or curdling will result.

Toasted sandwiches
Preheat a microwave browning dish on HIGH for 6 minutes.

Make sandwiches (such as ham and cheese) with the buttered side facing outwards.

Arrange on the browning dish and cook on HIGH for 30 seconds, then turn and cook for a further 30 seconds.

Vegetable stock
Slice 2 onions, toss them in a little olive oil and grill them until brown.

(This will give the stock colour and extra flavour without using salt.)

Place the onions in a casserole dish and add 2 sliced carrots, 1 sliced turnip, 1 cup chopped squash, 1½ cups spinach, ¨ cup chopped fresh dark mushrooms, 1 chopped celery stalk, 1 bay leaf, a pinch of tarragon and 3½ cups of water.

Cover and cook in the microwave on HIGH for about 20 minutes. Allow to stand for 20 minutes, strain and use.

White sauce
Place 2 tablespoons butter in a 4-cup jug. Cook on HIGH for 30-40 seconds. Stir in 2 tablespoons flour and salt and pepper.

Gradually add 1 cup milk and stir until smooth.

Cook on MEDIUM for 3-4 minutes, stirring every minute.

CAKES AND DESSERTS

CAKES AND DESSERTS

Microwaved cakes are light-textured and moist, and can be prepared in a fraction of the time it takes to bake them conventionally. However, some types of cake will not acquire a golden colour. So it is best to choose naturally moist recipes with ingredients that provide a good rich colour, such as chocolate or ginger, and to use wholemeal flour and brown sugar.

Most biscuits cannot be cooked in a microwave because they can only be cooked in small batches and they need to be turned often. However, biscuit slices, cooked in one slab and cut into slices after cooking, are ideal for microwave cooking.

Steamed puddings microwave exceptionally well with excellent results. Other favourite sweet things, such as meringues, crêpes, loaf cakes, Christmas puddings and milk puddings, also microwave successfully.

Biscuits

Biscuit mixtures need to be firm to be microwaved successfully.

Avoid mixtures with a high butter content.

Stand biscuits on waxed paper for cooking. Use a try or a piece of cardboard to transport them to and from the oven.

Biscuits should not be pressed down before cooking as they spread rapidly.

Stop cooking when the surface is dry. Overcooked biscuits will burn in the middle. Biscuits should look dry all over but still be soft to the touch when taken from the oven.

Leave biscuits to cool briefly before moving them to a cooling rack. They will also crisp at this time.

See also Slices

Bread

Bread will not have a crisp crust because microwave cooking draws moisture to the surface and prevents it from becoming crisp.

It is easy, however, to brown the loaf under a hot grill after cooking.

To give microwaved bread some colour, use whole-meal flour.

Breadcrumbs

To dry breadcrumbs in a microwave, spread them on a plate lined with absorbent kitchen paper and cook on HIGH until they are dry, stirring occasionally (about 3-4 minutes). Cool and store in a polythene bag.

Bread dough

You can use a microwave to speed up the rising of bread dough, but watch it all the time to prevent the dough from becoming too hot and killing the yeast.

Place the dough in a large bowl, cover with a large tea towel and cook on HIGH for 15 seconds, then leave to stand for 5 minutes.

Repeat the process several times until the dough springs back when pressed lightly with the fingertips.

Burned patches

If one large patch of a cake or loaf cake is burned, your oven has a hot spot and you should turn cakes frequently during cooking.

Lumpy sugar added to the mixture can cause burned patches throughout a cake. The lumps of sugar get very hot during cooking and result in burned patches.

Too much dried fruit in the cake mixture can also cause burned patches.

Dried fruit contains a lot of sugar and has the same effect as lumps of sugar. Try cutting down on the amount of fruit or try washing the fruit before coating it in flour.

To much sugar in the cake mixture is another cause of burned patches. Cut down on the sugar in the recipe.

Cakes

Microwaved cakes do not brown as they do in conventional cooking. To give a cake some brown colour, try using cocoa powder, brown sugar, spices or wholemeal flour in the mixture, or ice the finished cake.

Cake mixtures must be softer for microwave cooking than for conventional cooking. Add an extra egg or a further 15 ml/1 tablespoon milk for each egg used.

Avoid overbeating when adding dry ingredients as this leads to overrising and cakes falling apart. Use a fork to mix the ingredients.

A plastic cake container will not need greasing to be microwaved unless the mixture contains very little fat.

Other types of container, however, should be greased, and the base of larger containers should be lined with greaseproof paper.

Do not flour cake containers as this will produce an unpalatable coating on the cake.

A ring mould is the best type of container for microwaving cakes. It allows penetration of microwaves from all sides and the cake cooks evenly.

Cakes not cooked in a ring mould should be raised on a roasting rack so that microwaves can penetrate the cake from all sides during cooking.

Cake containers must be no more than half full before cooking because cakes rise

high in microwave cooking, so make sure that you use one large enough.

Choose a MEDIUM HIGH setting for most cake mixtures.

Very wet mixtures or those with a high fruit content need to be cooked on a lower setting for a longer time.

Even if the oven has a turntable or stirrer, cakes that rise unevenly should be repositioned during cooking to ensure even cooking.

As the cake approaches being cooked, cook for very small amounts of time.

Thirty seconds to a minute will have an effect on the result.

To test whether a cake is done, remove from the oven while still moist in areas on the surface (which would normally appear to be underdone).

The cooking will be completed during the standing time by the conduction of heat. Loaf cakes with a heavier texture should look dry on the surface.

If a cake is dry, it has been overcooked. Reduce cooking time in future.

See also Cupcakes, Loaf cakes

Chocolate

Chocolate melts perfectly in the microwave oven.

Break the chocolate into small pieces (unless using chocolate chips) and cook on LOW until it is soft and glossy on top (about 4 minutes).

Melting times vary, so check every minute during melting, and take care as chocolate burns easily.

Remove from the oven and stir until melted.

Do not overcook chocolate because it becomes thick, grainy, dull and difficult to handle.

Christmas pudding

A Christmas pudding can be microwaved in only 45 minutes. However, because traditional recipes contain a lot of sugar, dried fruits, fat and alcohol, all of which attract microwave energy and quickly reach a high temperature, great care must be taken not to burn the pudding.

MEDIUM LOW is the ideal setting.

A Christmas pudding must be watched during micro-wave cooking.

Add only 30 ml/2 table-spoons of your recipe's alcohol to the pudding mixture and replace the remaining liquid with milk or orange juice.

In order to keep the pudding moist, extra liquid is also required. Allow an extra 15 ml/1 tablespoon milk for each egg used.

Colour

To colour the tops of microwaved cakes, sprinkle a mixture of cinnamon and sugar or cinnamon and toasted coconut over the surface before serving.

Ingredients such as chocolate, coffee, carrot, dates or banana will add colour to a cake.

Confectionery and toppings

Almost any confectionery recipe can be adapted by using a microwave method and time. No change in ingredients is needed.

Select a large heat-proof container for sugary mixtures, which boil high. The utensil should be two or three times larger than the volume of the mixture.

Never cover the container.

Stir confectionery and sauces a few times during cooking. Frequent stirring is not necessary because the mixture will not scorch.

Stir the mixture with a long-handled wooden spoon to avoid being splattered.

Select HIGH for sugary syrups and fruit mixtures. Reduce power for chocolate, which is sensitive to microwave energy.

Use a special microwave confectionery thermometer or the old-fashioned cold water test for confectionery. Do not use a conventional confectionery thermometer inside the microwave oven.

Cooling

Cool cakes directly on the bench top. Heat trapped

between the dish and the bench top helps to complete cooking on the bottom of the cake.

A few moist spots on the surface of the cake will dry as cake cools.

Creaming

Creaming ingredients is easy. Simply soften the butter in the microwave on HIGH for 30-40 seconds before adding the sugar.

Crêpes

To make crêpes, whisk together 2 eggs (room temperature), $1/4$ cup milk (room temperature) and 1 tablespoon wholemeal flour.

Spray a 23-cm glass pie dish with vegetable cooking spray and pour in 3 tablespoons of the batter. Tip the dish until a 12-15 cm crêpe has formed.

Microwave, uncovered, on MEDIUM until cooked — about 2 minutes 40 seconds.

Flip the crêpe out, face side down, on to waxed paper and repeat with the remaining batter. Spray the dish each time. Makes 4 crêpes.

Crumb crusts

To make an excellent crumb crust for sweet flans, crush a 250 g packet malted biscuits and mix in

250 g melted butter and
1 teaspoon cinnamon.

Press into a greased 22-25
cm pie dish and microwave
on HIGH for 2 minutes.
Chill before use.

Cupcakes

If you are making a full-
sized cake and have some
batter left over (because
microwaved cakes should
never fill more than half the
container before cooking),
use the extra to make
cupcakes.

It's a good idea to use two
paper cups per cupcake for
extra support.

A number of small cakes
should be arranged in a
circle, with no cake in the
centre, to ensure even
penetration of microwaves
and therefore even cooking.

Custard

When making custard,
choose a dish with a small
diameter and a taller side.
This will prevent lumps
forming or the custard
boiling over during
cooking.

To make custard, mix
together 15 ml caster sugar,
30 ml custard powder and
a dash from 600 ml milk.

Heat the remaining milk on
HIGH for 4-5 minutes,
then pour it over the
custard powder and stir
well.

Return the mixture to the oven and cook on HIGH for 1-1½ minutes, stirring frequently.

Doneness
Microwave-cooked cakes leave the sides of the dish when cooked, and any moist spots on the surface will dry during standing time.

Dryness
If your cake or loaf is too dry, it could be over-cooked.

When in doubt, underbake rather than overbake. You can always put the cake back in the oven for a few seconds if necessary.

Microwave-cooked cakes need more moisture than conventionally cooked cakes. Add another egg or an extra 15 ml/1 table-spoon milk for every egg used.

If there is an uncooked circle of mixture on the base of the cake, try standing the cake on a roasting rack or upturned plate during cooking. The bottom of a deep cake or loaf cake cooks the most slowly.

Fudge
Place 100 g butter, 100 g plain chocolate, 500 g icing sugar and 50 ml/3 tablespoons milk in a large heatproof bowl.

Cook on HIGH for 3 minutes until the chocolate has melted, then beat vigorously with a wooden spoon until thick and creamy.

Pour into a shallow container and leave until set. Cut into squares when cold.

Gelatine
To dissolve gelatine, sprinkle it into the measured cold water according to the instructions on the packet and leave to soak and swell for 1 minute. Then cook on HIGH for 30-35 seconds until dissolved, stirring frequently. Do not boil.

Honey
When honey has crystallised, you can restore its texture by microwaving it on HIGH for 1-2 minutes in its glass jar without the lid.

Ice cream
Rock-hard ice cream can be softened very easily in the microwave — obviously with great care!

A 1-litre tub straight from the freezer should be microwaved on LOW for about 2 minutes.

Jelly
Jelly crystals can be dissolved in the microwave.

Simply put the crystals in a jug or bowl with about 150 ml cold water.

Cook on HIGH for 1½-2½ minutes until melted, then stir until dissolved.

Test jelly for doneness with a metal spoon.

Two large drops on the edge of the spoon should run together to form a single drop.

Loaf cakes

Use your favourite loaf recipes in the microwave oven, but substitute wholemeal flour for white flour, brown sugar for white and treacle for golden syrup in order to give the cake more colour.

Avoid over-mixing once dry ingredients have been added.

Always line the base of the dish with waxed paper, but do not grease the dish.

Shield the ends of the loaf dish with foil for the first 5-8 minutes of cooking in order to avoid overcooking.

Loaf cakes should be elevated on a rack or upturned pie plate during microwave cooking.

When the loaf is sufficiently cooked, stand it on a wooden surface for 5-10 minutes before turning out on to a cake cooler.

When completely cool, store in an airtight tin.

Always store loaf cakes for a day before slicing.

A loaf cake with dry ends and a moist centre will have cooked for too long. The ends cook much faster than the centre.

When the centre rises, test to see whether it is cooked.

Some loaf cakes benefit from being cooked on a MEDIUM setting, and this could be the remedy for a moist centre and dry ends.

Loaf cakes need to be turned during cooking to ensure even cooking. If the cake rises unevenly, turn it during cooking.

Meringue

Place 1 egg white in a medium-sized bowl and whisk lightly with a fork. Gradually sift in about 275–300 g icing sugar (depending on the size of the egg) and mix to give a very firm, non-sticky but pliable mixture.

Roll the mixture into small balls about the size of a walnut. Place a sheet of greaseproof paper in the base of the microwave oven or on the turntable and arrange 8 balls of the mixture in a circle on the paper, spacing them well apart.

Cook on HIGH for 1½ minutes until the mixture has puffed up. Cool meringues on a wire rack.

Repeat until all the mixture is used.

Mixing

Do not use a mixer to mix batters intended for microwave cooking. Instead combine the ingredients using a whisk or fork.

There is no need to mix the mixture until smooth for microwaving, and incorporating too

much air in the batter will make it go stale prematurely.

Pastry

Do not attempt to cook pastry other than sweet short crust or short crust in a microwave oven.

Pastry will not brown in a microwave oven. To give it colour, either use wholemeal flour or add a few drops of food colouring.

Pastry must be thoroughly chilled before cooking in order to avoid excessive shrinkage.

Microwaved pastry also tends not to be crisp. Rolling it out very thin or overcooking it very slightly will make it crisper.

Prick the pie shell generously to prevent shrinking.

Pastry will only be successful in the microwave oven if it is precooked before the filling is added.

Check for doneness by looking through the bottom of a glass dish. The crust should be dry and flaky.

Recipe conversion

Rich cakes using whole eggs adapt well to microwaving. Add an extra egg to a 1- or 2-egg cake.

If your recipe already calls for 3 eggs, reduce liquid by about a third.

Less reduction of liquid is needed if you bake your layer cake recipe in a ring-shaped dish.

Use a microwave recipe as a guide to time and power levels.

To convert recipes for single-crust pies, prepare and microwave the pie shell first. Then add filling and microwave again.

Timing for fruit pies depends on the type of fruit. Check for doneness after about 10 minutes.

Filling should be hot and
starting to cook in the
centre. It will complete
cooking as it cools during
standing time.

Double-crust pies cannot
be microwaved because the
bottom crust will not cook
properly.

Your microwave oven
simplifies the preparation
of puddings and custards as
well as precooked fillings
for cream, chiffon and
marshmallow pies. HIGH
softens gelatine in 1-2
minutes or melts marsh-
mallows in 2-4 minutes.

Use a microwave recipe as
a guide to method and time
for custards and creams.

Rice pudding

Place 50 g short-grain
white rice in a large bowl
and stir in 25 g sugar and
600 ml milk.

Cover the bowl and cook
on HIGH for 8-10 minutes
until boiling.

Stir well and cook on
MEDIUM LOW for 30
minutes, stirring every 10
minutes. Allow to stand
for 5 minutes.

Scones

Scones rise well, but always
follow a recipe designed
specifically for microwave
cooking.

Using wholemeal flour
improves the colour.

Preheat a browning dish on HIGH for 6-7 minutes. Sift 2 cups self-raising flour, 1 tablespoon sugar and a pinch of salt in a large mixing bowl. Rub 2 tablespoons butter into the flour until it resembles fine breadcrumbs. Make a well in the centre, add ¾ cup milk and mix to form a soft dough. Spread out dough with fingers until about 3 cm thick and cut out. Add 1 tablespoon butter and the scones to the browning dish. Cook on HIGH for 2 minutes. Turn and cook on HIGH for a further 2-3 minutes.

Shortbread
Shortbread is very difficult to microwave successfully.

It tends to be pale and the centre may burn.

It is best cooked in a conventional oven.

Sifting
When making cakes for microwave cooking, there is no need to sift dry ingredients.

Slices
Your favourite slice recipes can be cooked in the microwave oven.

Use a rectangular dish, and remember that dish size influences cooking time — a larger dish requires more time, and a smaller dish requires less time.

The dish may be lightly greased if required.

Cook slices on MEDIUM HIGH unless the mixture is particularly wet. When the mixture is a wet one, use MEDIUM.

Continue cooking until the slice is dry all over but still soft. Allow to stand; the slice will become crisp while cooling.

Do not cut the slice while it is still warm or it will crumble.

If the slice doesn't come out of its dish easily, stand the dish in a tray of hot water for a minute of two until the slice loosens.

Slices should be crisp. If your slice has a soft texture, the cooking time has been too short. If the slice is hard, reduce the cooking time in future.

Softening sugar
Sugar that has become hard can be softened in a microwave oven.

Put the sugar, in its original wrapper, in the oven on HIGH for 30-40 seconds.

Soft fillings
Quiche fillings and baked custard can be tested by inserting a knife a third of the way in from the edge. The knife should be clean when withdrawn.

Stand cooked custard in cold water when cooking is complete to cool and stop further cooking.

Soufflés

Soufflés can be micro-waved, but they are not as successful as those prepared in a conventional oven.

They rise and fall several times during microwave cooking and fall quickly when removed from the oven, and they do not form a crust.

Steamed pudding

Steamed puddings can microwaved in a fraction of the time needed for conventional steaming, and the results are excellent. Follow your favourite recipe and either cook it in a soufflé dish or Pyrex bowl. Cook uncovered on MEDIUM for 6-8 minutes. Stand, covered, for 5 minutes before turning out.

Sweets *See* Confectionery and toppings

Water bath

Desserts that usually require cooking in a water bath in the conventional oven will cook well without this treatment in a microwave oven.

DEFROSTING

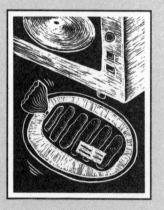

Frozen food can be defrosted in minutes in a microwave oven rather than hours by conventional means.
There is no need to plan meals long in advance, and
you can cope with such contingencies as unexpected
visitors.

Defrosting with a microwave requires some care. If
frozen food is subjected to a continuous period of
microwave energy the areas which have melted first
begin to heat up while adjacent parts remain frozen.
The result is hot and frozen food in the same dish.
Better results will be obtained when there are rests
between bursts of microwaving. The rest period allows
warmth from the defrosted food to be conducted to the
frozen areas and help to ensure even defrosting.

Many microwave ovens incorporate a LOW or
DEFROST setting. This useful feature automatically
switches the power on and off.

After defrosting, food needs to stand before cooking or reheating. As with the standing time after

microwave cooking, this standing time is an essential part of the defrosting process. Without standing time food might be unevenly defrosted, dry out on the edges or start cooking.

Bacon

To defrost bacon, allow 2-3 minutes per 250 g on a DEFROST setting.

Separate the rashers halfway through defrosting.

Beef

To defrost boned joints of beef, allow 8-10 minutes per 500 g on a DEFROST setting. Turn the meat halfway through defrosting, and allow to stand for 15 minutes.

To defrost joints on the bone, allow 10-12 minutes per 500 g on a DEFROST setting. Shield any thinner bone portions with foil, and turn over halfway through. Allow 30 minutes standing time.

To defrost minced beef, allow 8-10 minutes per 500 g on a DEFROST setting. Turn and remove outside pieces of meat halfway through defrosting time.

To defrost cubed beef,
allow 6-8 minutes per
500 g on a DEFROST
setting. Rearrange the meat
halfway through.

To defrost beef steaks,
allow 8-10 minutes per
500 g on a DEFROST
setting, and turn over
halfway through.

To defrost beef rissoles,
allow 5 minutes for 4
rissoles, 10 minutes for
8 and 15 minutes for 12
on a DEFROST setting.
Rearrange and turn the
rissoles over halfway
through.

Cakes
Cakes, bread and bread
products, buns, scones,

biscuits and pastry items
should be placed on
absorbent kitchen paper
to absorb moisture during
defrosting.

Chicken
To defrost a whole chicken,
remove the chicken from
the plastic bag and elevate
on a roasting rack in the
oven. Use the DEFROST
setting.

Allow 6-8 minutes per
500 g for a whole chicken,
and turn halfway through.

Remove the giblets and
clean inside and out with
cold running water when
defrosted.

Chicken pieces
Use a DEFROST setting
and allow 5-7 minutes per

500 g when defrosting
chicken pieces.

Separate and rearrange the
pieces during defrosting.

Covering
Covering is not strictly
necessary, but it will help
to speed up defrosting,
particularly of cooked
dishes.

Crayfish or crab
Whole crayfish or crab
should be defrosted for
6-8 minutes per 500 g on
a DEFROST setting.

Turn crayfish or crab
halfway through, then
stand for 10 minutes.

Crab claws or crayfish tails
should be defrosted for

5-6 minutes per 500 g
on a DEFROST setting.
Separate and rearrange
during defrosting, and
stand for 10 minutes.

Defrosting food — general hints
Only defrost food in the
microwave oven if it is to
be cooked and eaten
immediately.

When freezing cooked
meals, use a dish that is
suitable for both
microwave defrosting
and reheating.

Meals frozen in foil
containers can be
defrosted and reheated
in the microwave oven,
provided that the
container is no more

than 3 cm deep and the foil lid is removed.

Cartons of food should be opened.

For faster and more even defrosting, separate frozen foods, such as chops and fish cutlets, into pieces as they defrost.

Turn food over if possible during defrosting. If this is not possible, rearrange individual items or turn the dish around.

Shake or gently break down fruit during the defrosting and standing time.

Flex pouches and packagings that cannot be broken up or stirred in order to distribute the heat evenly.

Dishes
If frozen food has to be placed in a dish, match the size and shape of the dish to the size and shape of the food.

Duck
To defrost a whole duck, allow 6-8 minutes per 500 g on a DEFROST setting.

Turn the duck halfway through the defrosting time.

Remove the giblets and clean inside and out with cold running water when defrosted.

Elevate the food

Frozen meat and large cooked dishes should be elevated on a rack set in a dish for defrosting. This will allow even defrosting and prevent meat from sitting in its own liquid.

Fat

Fat attracts more microwave energy than meat, so always trim away as much fat as possible from meat before freezing to ensure even defrosting.

Fish

Whole white fish or fillets should be defrosted for 3-4 minutes per 500 g on a DEFROST setting.

Turn whole fish or fillets halfway through the defrosting time, and allow to stand for 10 minutes afterwards.

Before defrosting, cover any thin parts that might start to cook with foil.

Separate fish fillets as they begin to defrost.

When almost defrosted, run cold water over fish to complete the defrosting process.

Foil

If large items of food begin to defrost unevenly, small pieces of foil may be used to cover any areas that appear to be developing hot spots or beginning to cook.

Foil trays

Food can be defrosted in foil trays which are no deeper than 3 cm.

Freezer bags

Before defrosting meat, remove the freezer bag or wrap to prevent the meat sitting in its own liquid, which will otherwise boil, causing the defrosting meat to stew.

To remove frozen meat from the freezer wrap or bag, defrost for a few minutes until the wrap or bag is easily removed.

Remove metal twist ties from freezer bags to prevent arcing.

Joints of meat

Start defrosting a joint of meat in its wrapper, first piercing it, and remove it as soon as possible — usually after a quarter of its defrosting time.

Place the joint on a microwave roasting rack.

If the joint shows signs of cooking during defrosting, rest it for about 20 minutes.

A joint is defrosted when a skewer can easily pass through the thickest part of the meat.

Lamb and veal

To defrost boned joints of lamb or veal, allow 8-10 minutes per 500 g on a

DEFROST setting. Turn the meat over halfway through defrosting time, and allow to stand for 15 minutes.

To defrost joints of lamb or veal on the bone, allow 8-10 minutes per 500 g on a DEFROST setting. Shield any thinner portions with foil, and turn over halfway through. Stand for 30 minutes.

To defrost minced lamb or veal, allow 8-10 minutes per 500 g on a DEFROST setting. Turn the meat and remove outside pieces halfway through.

To defrost lamb or veal chops, allow 8-10 minutes per 500 g on a DEFROST setting, separate and rearrange the chops halfway through.

Meat

Always remove meat from its polystyrene tray before defrosting.

Meat arranged in a single layer will defrost more quickly and evenly than meat stacked in several layers. Interleaving cuts with freezer wrap will make it easier to separate them before defrosting.

Always arrange the individual cuts around the outside of the dish, with the meatiest portions positioned at the edges.

Rearrange the meat during the defrosting period.

Large cuts of meat will take longer to defrost than small cuts.

To ensure even defrosting of joints or roasts, divide the total defrosting time into three sections and allow 5-10 minutes standing time between each section.

Pastry
A 250 g packet of shortcrust or puff pastry should be defrosted on the LOW or DEFROST setting for 1 minute, then left to stand for 20 minutes.

A 400 g packet needs 2 minutes in the oven and 20-30 minutes standing time.

Pierce skins
Pierce the skins of such frozen foods as sausages before defrosting.

Pork
To defrost boned joints of pork, place the meat in a microwave oven on a DEFROST setting for 8-10 minutes per 500 g. Turn over halfway though defrosting and stand for 15 minutes.

To defrost pork tenderloin and chops, allow 8-10 minutes per 500 g on a DEFROST setting.

Separate and rearrange the meat halfway through and

allow to stand for 10
minutes.

To defrost pork sausages,
allow 5-6 minutes per
500 g on a DEFROST
setting. Separate and
rearrange the sausages
halfway through. Leave
to stand for 10 minutes.

Poultry
Finish defrosting poultry in
cold water, rather than try
to thaw it completely with
microwave energy;
otherwise it might start to
cook around the outside
before it is fully defrosted
in the centre.

Remember to remove
giblets from defrosted
poultry before
cooking.

Prawns and shrimps
Prawns and shrimps
should be defrosted for 4-6
minutes per 500 g on a
DEFROST setting.

Separate and rearrange
during defrosting, then
stand for 2 minutes.

Plunge into cold water to
prevent cooking, drain and
pat dry.

Shape
Flat packages of food will
defrost more quickly and
effectively than thick
packages of the same
weight.

Soup
Pour soup that is to be
frozen into single-portion

containers so that it can be defrosted in the microwave more quickly than a large quantity.

Standing time

Remember the defrosting process will continue during the standing time.

Do not attempt to defrost foods completely in a microwave; otherwise the outer edges will dry out or even begin to cook.

Temperature

Food taken from the deep-freeze will need more time to defrost than that taken from the freezer compartment of the refrigerator.

Refrigerated and frozen food will take longer to reheat than food at room temperature. Frozen food requires the longest time.

When reheating, ensure that food is initially too hot to eat. If in doubt, return to the microwave for a little longer.

A useful test is to touch the base of the cooking dish after taking it out of the oven. If the centre is cold, so is the food.

Main courses and meat dishes benefit from more gentle heating on low rather than high settings, especially if they have been refrigerated.

Cover tightly during reheating.

Testing

Test chops and steak during thawing by pressing the surface with your fingers. The meat should feel cold to the touch and give in the thickest part.

Timing

Always underestimate defrosting times.

Many foods will still be icy in the centre when removed from the microwave, but will melt during the standing time.

If necessary, food can be returned to the microwave for further defrosting.

Turkey

To defrost a whole turkey, allow 10-12 minutes per 500 g on DEFROST, and turn the bird halfway through the defrosting time. Stand for 30 minutes, then place under cold running water.

Vegetables

Frozen vegetables are best cooked directly from the freezer without being defrosted.

REHEATING

Reheating food is simple with your microwave oven. Most food reheats without loss of colour, quality or flavour, and you will find you waste less food and use less fuel as well. Meals prepared in advance may be reheated later with no need to heat the conventional oven.

Reheating in the microwave oven is far more successful and tasty than conventional methods. There is little or no drying of food edges, and the speed of reheating gives harmful germs less chance to survive. In fact, the food will be as appealing and tasty as when it was first prepared.

However, some care needs to be taken. Reheating times will depend on the starting temperature of the food, for example, and overheating dries and toughens food, so it is better to underestimate rather than over-estimate reheating times. Other principles of microwave cooking, such as the need to cover food, the importance of positioning food correctly and the need to stir and turn food, also apply to reheating.

Baby food

Home-made baby food should be heated in suitable containers, and commercially prepared foods can be heated either in their glass jars with the lids removed or decanted from cans and other containers into microwave-safe dishes.

Always check all food and drink for babies to ensure that it is not too hot before serving.

Remember to allow standing time as both liquids and food will continue to heat up for a few minutes after being removed from the oven.

Batter

Fish in batter that has been fried conventionally will not reheat as well in a microwave oven as the batter goes soggy.

Bread

Wrap bread and bread products in absorbent kitchen paper to absorb moisture and do not overheat, otherwise they will toughen.

One bread roll will be warm in about 10 seconds.

Canned food

Canned food should be transferred to a suitable dish and covered during reheating.

Casseroles

Stir casseroles and main dishes if possible during reheating to distribute heat and shorten the reheating period.

Use a MEDIUM power setting.

Dishes that cannot be stirred should be shaken gently and rotated manually.

Containers

Place food to be reheated in a shallow container so that the microwaves can penetrate the food easily.

Do not use such a large dish that the sauce spreads thinly and burns.

Convenience foods

When heating convenience foods, the instructions should be regarded as a guide only, since micro-wave ovens and foods vary so much.

Before eating always check that the food is piping hot, not just warm.

To ensure even heating, stir food during cooking, and turn or rearrange foods that cannot be stirred.

After cooking, allow the food to stand so that all parts of the food become equally hot.

Use a thermometer to check that the temperature of the food has reached more than 70°C in all parts of the dish if you are not sure that the food has heated adequately. If necessary, return it to the oven for another minute.

Croissants
Croissants contain a lot of butter, which attracts microwave energy, so they can easily overcook or become soggy.

Wrap them in absorbent kitchen paper and heat on HIGH for 30 seconds (for two croissants).

Hollandaise sauce
To reheat hollandaise sauce, whisk 1-2 table-

spoons melted butter into the cold sauce.

Cook on MEDIUM for 30-60 seconds.

Lids
Remove all lids from jars and containers before reheating in a microwave oven.

Meat
Some pre-browned meats, including steaks, chops and patties (barbecued and frozen), may be reheated without defrosting.

Reheating times for pre-browned cuts of meat vary depending on required taste, thickness and degree of cooking when initially browned.

Metal ties

Remove metal twist ties from bags and replace with string or an elastic band before putting bags in the microwave.

Pancakes

To reheat pancakes, put slices of greaseproof paper between each one and cover them with it as well. The stack can be up to 8 pancakes high.

Cook on HIGH for 1-1½ minutes or until warmed through.

Pasta

To reheat 1 cup/250 ml spaghetti or linguine, cover tightly and microwave on HIGH until warmed thoroughly — about 1 minute. Sprinkle with freshly grated parmesan and allow to stand for 1 minute before serving.

A dish that cannot be stirred, such as lasagne, should be covered and reheated on LOW. On a higher setting the meat and cheese will toughen and the pasta will dry out.

Pastry

Pastry will go soft when reheated in a microwave oven unless you place it on a piece of absorbent kitchen paper.

Pies

Cooked pastry items reheat extremely quickly in the

microwave, especially if they have a sweet filling, such as fruit pies.

The outer pastry will feel barely warm, but the filling will be very hot — the heat will equalise during a few minutes standing time.

One mince pie, for example, will be heated in about 10 seconds.

The microwave oven should not be left unattended during these short reheating periods.

Plated meals

If you want to serve food on to a plate to reheat later, arrange it in an even layer, placing dense foods towards the outside of the plate and quicker heating foods in the centre.

Cover plate with a lid to retain heat and moisture.

Reheating food — general hints

Cover food to prevent it drying out.

Stir the food occasionally for even heating. Items that cannot be stirred should be turned or rearranged.

Reheating in a microwave oven is extremely quick, so care should be taken that small items of food do not overcook.

Cooked pastry and breads must be placed on absorbent kitchen paper to absorb moisture during reheating and prevent the bottom of the food from becoming soggy.

Fat and sugar attract microwaves and tend to cook before other ingredients.

The filling in sweet pies, for example, can be much hotter than the rest of the dish, but this difference will even out during standing time.

When reheating an entire meal on the same plate, keep the height of the various items as even as possible and arrange the more dense and thicker items towards the outside of the plate.

Rice

To reheat cold cooked rice, add 1 tablespoon water to the rice, cover and microwave on HIGH for 2-3 minutes.

Scones

Scones can be warmed in a microwave, but only in small quantities, and then they end up with a soft crust.

Wrap the scones loosely in a napkin or absorbent kitchen paper and cook on HIGH in 1 minute bursts or until just warm.

Eat the scones immediately or they will become hard.

Sliced meat

Thin slices of meat will heat more evenly than thickly cut slices.

Add sauce or gravy to provide moisture and prevent the meat from drying during reheating.

Soup

Soups will reheat faster as individual portions, either in a bowl or mug. Stir during reheating.

For the most even reheating process use a tall-sided dish with a small diameter.

To heat 1 serving of soup from the refrigerator allow 2½ minutes on HIGH. A frozen serving of soup will require 6-8 minutes, stirring once halfway through.

Don't use the microwave to reheat soups that contain milk because they can become too frothy.

Reheat soups on a MEDIUM LOW setting if they contain cream, seafood, mushrooms or pulses, but use a HIGH setting for all others.

Stacking ring

Using a stacking ring will enable you to heat more than one plate of food at a time. The food is heated when the bottom of the plate feels warm.

Take-away chicken

Before reheating a take-away chicken in the micro-wave, remove it from its foil-lined bag.

Vegetables

Vegetables in sauce reheat well in a covered dish. They should be stirred during reheating if possible; otherwise rotate the dish, especially in ovens without a turntable.

Care is needed to prevent overcooking when reheating some vegetables with sauce.

Fibrous vegetables such as broccoli spears and asparagus tend to lose texture and toughen when reheated.

Exercise care when reheating starchy vegetables such as jacket potatoes to prevent overcooking or dehydration.

— • NOTES • ——————